A LITTLE SPOT OF

FEELINGS

& EMOTIONS

Educator's Guide

HANDS-ON ACTIVITIES ○ LESSON PLANS ○ STEM ○ WORKSHEETS

DIANE ALBER

DISCLAIMER

This guide is not for commercial use. You cannot resell or distribute any part of this guide for any form of compensation.

You can print up to 30 copies of the printables in the back of the guide to be handed out to the class.

This PDF may NOT be distributed or shared with others.

If you would like to discuss school bulk discounts, print more copies, or use this guide in a class you charge for, please contact info@dianealber.com.

Check out more at www.dianealber.com
BOX SETS AVAILABLE AT DISCOUNTED RATE!

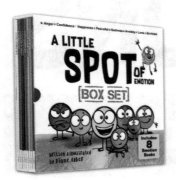

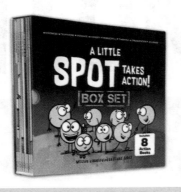

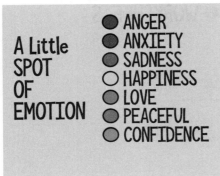

A Little SPOT OF EMOTION
- ANGER
- ANXIETY
- SADNESS
- HAPPINESS
- LOVE
- PEACEFUL
- CONFIDENCE

A Little SPOT TAKES ACTION
- Kindness
- Responsibility
- Patience
- Respect
- Honesty
- Organization
- Diversity
- Safety

A Little SPOT OF LIFE SKILLS
- Perseverance
- Courage
- Teamwork
- Talent
- Thankful
- Optimism
- Creativity
- Giving

ABOUT THE AUTHOR

Diane Alber has had a passion for art since she held her first crayon at age two, which inspired her to earn a Bachelor's in Fine Arts from Arizona State University. She is a wife and a mother of two young, energetic children who love books. She became inspired to start writing and illustrating books because she saw a need for a book that inspired art and creativity in children. Her series later evolved to cover topics that are hard to explain to children, like EMOTIONS, actions, and life skills. She hopes that her entire series inspires creativity and encourages children to become the best they can be!

CONTENTS

ACKNOWLEDGMENTS

A big THANK YOU to everyone who has supported me! I am forever grateful to all the teachers, art teachers, parents, and caregivers who offered suggestions for new products, provided advice, and gave me the encouragement to keep creating. Thank you for spreading the word about my brand. Without you, none of this would have been possible!

To Julie Marzano at Fine Motor Bootcamp (www.finemotorbootcamp.com), for being a great consultant while creating this guide.

A special thanks to Rachael, Hayley, Buddy, Erica, Rebecca, Julia, Adir, Karen, and Stacy, for listening to my late-night ideas and for offering fantastic advice.

I also want to thank my husband for believing in my ideas and letting me run with them! Also, a big THANK YOU to my mom who is the first to read every one of my books and who looks forward to reading any new ones. And finally, thanks to my amazing children, who have inspired me to do everything in this book including, all the worksheets and projects!

Diane Alber

What is Social-EMOTIONAL Learning?

Social-EMOTIONAL Learning (SEL) refers to the development of self-awareness, self-control, self-regulation, social skills, and responsible decision-making, all of which are essential for school and life successes.

This guide will give you thought-provoking lessons, discussions, and activities to help the students identify EMOTIONS. Students will learn how to handle overwhelming FEELINGS, develop a positive self-image, and learn how to improve social and EMOTIONAL skills needed to show empathy, compassion, and kindness. Over several weeks, students will learn seven EMOTIONS and the FEELINGS associated with them. They will learn managing techniques as well as coping strategies to regulate BIG EMOTIONS.

WHY USE SPOTS TO TEACH FEELINGS AND EMOTIONS?

We all experience FEELINGS and EMOTIONS every day. Learning when and why they show up can help you make friends, stay safe, motivate you, give you CONFIDENCE, and so much more!

SPOTS are easy to visualize, and if you can visualize your FEELINGS or EMOTIONS as a "thing," it can be easier to manage. You can employ self-talk to your "SPOTS" and learn times and places they might show up. For example, your CONFIDENCE SPOT grows when it receives POSITIVE REINFORCEMENT, and your ANGRY SPOT shrinks down to a PEACEFUL SPOT when you breathe. Thinking of EMOTIONS and FEELINGS as things make teaching and learning FEELINGS and EMOTIONS easier!

We've heard from numerous educators that they sometimes feel like they are on an island with very little help in sight. That is why we created this Educator Kit. We spent months talking with teachers, counselors, and homeschool parents, and listening to what they would need to make teaching EMOTIONS both educational and fun. Every item in the kit was carefully designed and selected to fit a specific need.

- EMOTION Box set (8 EMOTION Books)
- EMOTION Plush Set (8 EMOTION Plushies)
- 188 Page Educator Guide
- Digital Educator Guide

- 1 Set of Jumbo Flash Cards
- 1 Set of Regular Flash Cards
- 1 Sticker Book (1400 Stickers)
- 1 FEELINGS Book

FEELINGS AND EMOTION FLASH CARDS

We designed two different sizes of flashcards. The jumbo set can be used in a large group, classroom setting, or can be displayed on a board. The regular set is intended to be used for a smaller audience. It is great for a more personal experience or a smaller group (1-4 students). The set is wonderful for games and easier to store. We felt it was essential to include both sets to offer the educator options.

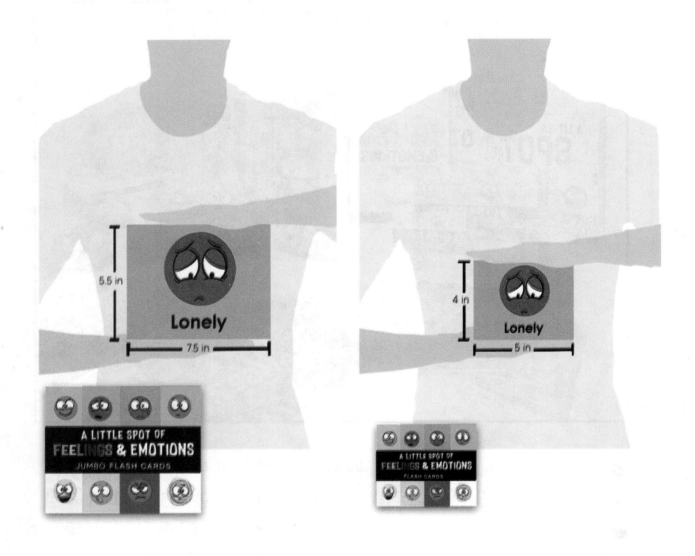

GAMES TO PLAY WITH FEELING AND EMOTION CARDS

● **Pick Out and Act Out:**
Have all the cards in a bucket and have the students pick out a card without looking. Have them act out the face, and give a situation when someone could experience that FEELING or EMOTION.

● **Conversation Cards:**
Ask the student to pick out how they are feeling from the pile of cards. Discuss choices.

● **Creative Writing:**
Hand out a card to every student, have them draw a situation that could cause that EMOTION. Write a story about that picture.

● **Memory Game:**
Pick out two EMOTIONS/FEELINGS of the same color. Have the student play a memory game.

● **Storytelling:**
Pass out two cards to each student. Have them write a story about a situation that includes those two FEELINGS/EMOTIONS.

● **Mirror:**
Have the student pick a card and create the face on the card in a mirror.

● **Headbands:**
Students will need to get into pairs. Place the cards face down in the middle of the playing area. Have both students place a headband on their head and take a card without them looking. Have them place the card in the center of their headband with the face side up. They must use words, situations, or faces to guess the color or EMOTION.

PLUSH TOYS

We wanted plushies that can be used as a communication tool, to encourage fun experiences, and to foster a connection. If students have a hard time verbally communicating, they can pick out the plushie that best represents how they FEEL. This adds another layer of teaching to help students retain more information.

PLUSH TOYS ACTIVITIES

● **Puppets:** The students can act out different EMOTIONS with the plushie.

● **Hiding HAPPINESS:** Hide the HAPPINESS plushie somewhere in the room. Once the students find it, explain how that little feeling of excitement is HAPPINESS!

● **Affirmations:** Students can sit around in a circle with one of them holding a CONFIDENCE SPOT. Then have that student tell a story or say a positive affirmation about themselves and pass the SPOT to the next student.

● **Calming Corner:** The plushies are great to use in a calming corner (see page 46).

SPOT STICKER BOOK

We wanted to provide an easy self-contained art project. This SPOT sticker book is used several times throughout the guide and it has enough stickers for an entire class. Each sticker sheet can be cut into quarters for easy distribution to the students.

Most of the guide activities require minimal materials beyond the Educator Kit and the educator can make substitutions when necessary. Additional books that are not included in the kit, but are used in this guide are listed below.

Educator Kit and extension books are available as a discounted bundle on www.dianealber.com

HOW TO USE THIS BOOK

This book is divided into three parts: Part One contains an EMOTION OVERVIEW consisting of learning topics. Part Two contains EMOTION EXPLORATION, and Part Three contains the handouts and supplemental materials for the educator to use with Part One and Part Two. Part One provides a brief overview of all the EMOTIONS, and Part Two focuses on each EMOTION separately. Each lesson, learning topic, and specific EMOTION EXPLORATION refers to a children's picture book that reflects the respective section's content. The book icon indicates when the educator should be reading the book and what section to refer to.

Educator Reading

Discussion

Also included in each section is a hands-on arts and crafts activity so the students can play while they learn. This makes learning more meaningful and memorable. By using multiple senses, the students can use more of their brain, which leads them to be more engaged and retain more information.

Hands-on: Worksheets

Hands-on: Arts and Crafts

Learning objective

We also included worksheets for an additional learning method that is simple and can be for distance learners. The worksheets can help with fine motor development and are beneficial for students with a shorter attention span. This Educator Guide was designed to be used by both novice educators and those with years of classroom experience. Areas presented in red text are intended to serve as the educator's script, if needed, for teaching the lesson.

GUIDE OUTLINE

Grade level(s): Kindergarten-2nd

This guide was created adhering to Common Core standards and CASEL: Effective Social-EMOTIONAL Learning Programs. It was developed to be a fun and creative resource to teach FEELINGS & EMOTIONS to elementary school students. The activities and lessons are created for 5-8 year olds, but can easily be adapted for younger or older students.

FEELINGS & EMOTIONS

LEARNING OBJECTIVES

Students will:

- Identify similarities and differences between themselves and others.
- Associate EMOTIONS with facial expressions, body language, and words.
- Identify, express, and describe their FEELINGS and those of others.
- Learn how to manage and self-regulate FEELINGS and EMOTIONS.
- Learn how to use color to express EMOTIONS.

The educator might note that there is some repetition in the lessons and objectives; that was intended specifically to help reinforce key concepts.

TEACHING TIPS

Several steps can be taken to make this Educator Guide successful in the classroom:

- Read the lesson in its entirety before teaching the class.
- Use creativity and adapt to any lesson that would fit the classroom.
- Be inspiring to the students by motivating them and being positive.
- Model the new EMOTIONAL skills learned as often as possible in other subjects.

SEL (CASEL SEL FRAMEWORK)

● Concept 1: Self-Awareness

Students develop a sense of personal identity as they recognize the characteristics that make them unique as individuals. Students can start identifying FEELINGS in themselves and others.

● Concept 2: Recognize and Express FEELINGS

Students develop an awareness of their FEELINGS as well as FEELINGS in others through daily interactions with peers and adults. Children develop the ability to effectively and appropriately express themselves and learn that their FEELINGS and the FEELINGS of others are important.

● Concept 3: Social Awareness

Students develop the ability to recognize the FEELINGS they are having. They will learn mindfulness to focus on the present and empathize with others.

● Concept 4: Relationship Skills

Students develop the ability to communicate clearly and listen when needed.

● Concept 5: Self-Management Skills

Students will learn managing and coping techniques.

FINE ARTS (VISUAL ARTS STANDARDS)

● Concept 1: Create and Understand Visual Arts.

Students will learn how to use a wide variety of materials to demonstrate personal interpretations of feelings, thoughts, and ideas.

ENGLISH LANGUAGE ARTS (COMMON CORE STANDARDS)

● **Concept 1: Key Ideas and Details**
Students will identify key details in stories and understand lessons.

● **Concept 2: Craft and Structure**
Students will start to identify unknown words that suggest FEELINGS or appeal to the senses.

● **Concept 3: Vocabulary**
Students will identify new meanings for familiar words and apply them accurately and determine the meaning of unknown words.

● **Concept 4: Text Types and Purposes**
Students will use a combination of drawing and dictation to compose information.

SEL INTEGRATING MATH & SCIENCE (COMMON CORE STANDARDS)

Lesson plans will integrate discussion prompts and student reflection using various math and science projects to provide hands-on learning.

● **Concept 1: Geometry**
Students will learn how to identify and describe shapes. Analyze, compare, create, and compose shapes.

● **Concept 2: Patterns**
Students will learn how use their senses to make observations about patterns.

NOTES:

_____

_____

_____

_____

_____

_____

_____

_____

_____

_____

_____

_____

_____

_____

_____

_____

PART ONE: EMOTION OVERVIEW

○ EMOTIONAL Vocabulary
○ EMOTIONAL Awareness
○ EMOTION Check-In
○ Mixed EMOTIONS

○ Colors and EMOTIONS/FEELINGS
○ Facial Expressions and Body Language
○ Connection Between FEELINGS and EMOTIONS
○ How Am I Feeling?

EMOTIONALLY intelligent students have the ability to effectively communicate how they are feeling and can recognize FEELINGS in others. They are able to identify cause and effect in their negative attitude and behavior, and are able to deal with whatever life throws at them. The students are able to choose how they respond to conflict and have the skills necessary to reach their full potential.

TEACHING TIPS

○ Set clear expectations on how to behave in the classroom.
○ Get to know your students and how they express EMOTIONS.
○ During core subjects, students can attempt to use coping skills and identify EMOTIONS.

Learning objective

Educator Reading

Discussion

Hands-on: Arts and Crafts

Hands-on: Worksheets

Reminder: Areas presented in red text are intended to serve as the educator's script, if needed, for teaching the lesson.

EMOTIONS & FEELINGS INTRODUCTION

EMOTIONS and FEELINGS are usually used together, but knowing the difference is important. EMOTIONS usually come after a series of FEELINGS. If the students can understand when they are frustrated, they can prevent themselves from experiencing ANGER. Ask students to share how they are FEELING today. Explain that they will learn more about how they can recognize the FEELINGS and EMOTIONS they are having.

Ask the students to describe a time they had an EMOTION or FEELING. What do FEELINGS and EMOTIONS do for us? One way they can help is to motivate us to do something. For example: Imagine you feel SAD for someone who is sitting alone. What might you do? You might have avoided that person altogether, but since you felt sorry for them, you went over to say hello. As you learn to manage your EMOTIONS, you can learn that they can help you make friends and accomplish more goals.

EMOTIONAL VOCABULARY

When students are asked how they are doing, the usual response is "good." The goal is to help students communicate more meaningfully, using language that reflects a range of FEELINGS.

Learning Objective:

○ Students will learn new vocabulary that describes their FEELINGS and EMOTIONS.

Select the flashcards depicting EMOTIONS. Cover the name of the EMOTION, and ask students to identify FEELINGS associated with that EMOTION. Each EMOTION in PART TWO of this guide will have a web printout for the kids to fill out.

Appendix 161   Appendix 167

EMOTIONAL AWARENESS

When students develop a strong EMOTIONAL tool kit, they can easily manage life's ups and downs.

 Learning Objective:

○ Students will learn to recognize FEELINGS and EMOTIONS in themselves and others.

For students to manage their FEELINGS and EMOTIONS, they must understand them. Pages 98 and 99 describe additional ways to use the flashcards.

Use these flashcards so students can brainstorm how FEELINGS and EMOTIONS can help them; an example would be: Nervous: You might be worried about a test. This motivates you to study more.

EMOTION CHECK-IN

These check-ins are designed to help students to slow down and get an accurate read of how they are FEELING. This helps the students identify how they truly FEEL and determine whether they want to FEEL that way.

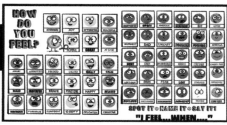

Appendix 108-109

 Learning Objective:

○ Students will learn the benefits of FEELINGS and EMOTION check-ins.

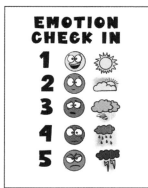

Appendix 110

Sometimes it's hard to tell how you are FEELING. Over the next couple of weeks, you will be learning all about FEELINGS and EMOTIONS. Introduce the Check-In Charts. When you understand how you FEEL, it's easier to self-regulate. Every day try and take a moment to think about how you are FEELING and why you are FEELING that way.

 Learning Objective:

Students will learn:

○ How to identify EMOTIONS when they are happening simultaneously.

Materials Needed:

○ Jumbo Flashcards

Happiness

Sadness

Hold up two different EMOTION cards:

Explain that we can feel two EMOTIONS at the same time. We can feel HAPPY that summer break is coming, and also SAD because we won't see our friends every day. We experience EMOTIONS and FEELINGS all the time, and sometimes we become ANGRY with someone, and we aren't even sure why. Learning to identify our FEELINGS can prevent that from happening. We are all unique, we all come from diverse backgrounds, and have experienced different situations. For example, if I assign an extra book to read today about bugs, some of the class may be excited about learning more about bugs, and some students may be annoyed because they think they are gross.

I'm going to give you scenarios, and I want you to tell me how you would FEEL:

You wake up late for school.

You are given a dinner plate of food you don't want to eat.

Your teacher calls on you, and you don't know the answer.

You hear someone say something mean about you.

Your friend won't share a toy.

Your grandparents are visiting.

COLORS AND EMOTIONS/FEELINGS

 Learning Objective:

Students will learn:

○ New vocabulary to describe FEELINGS and EMOTIONS.
○ How to associate colors with FEELINGS and EMOTIONS.

Reading:

A Little Scribble SPOT by Diane Alber.
Introduce the book to the students.

This book will help teach us about FEELINGS and EMOTIONS. Can you name some you've had before? Let the students think for a moment, then have them share their ideas with the class. Write the ideas down on chart paper or the board. Next to the ideas, draw a face that shows that FEELING or EMOTION. Use one of the plushies to have the students make their bodies/faces look like that. (Show me _____.) Some ideas they might have: happy, sad, mad, scared, excited, shy. Scribble SPOT, is the main character of the book. As I read the book, we'll think and talk about how Scribble is FEELING. We will also discuss specific colors that are associated with FEELINGS and EMOTIONS, too!

Appendix 160

 Scribble SPOT Activity:

Pass out the worksheet on Appendix 160 and ask the students to scribble the colors they think Scribble is FEELING.

Read until: "It's healthy to experience EMOTIONS! But when they get all jumbled together, it's hard to know exactly how you are FEELING, and that can make you become frustrated or confused." Have you ever felt confused or frustrated?

Try separating your FEELINGS and EMOTIONS out like this, so they will be easier to identify. Can colors make us FEEL a certain way? Scribble seven circles on the board. Have the students give some examples: blue=SAD, red=ANGER, yellow=HAPPY

Appendix 185

ANGER
FRUSTRATED
MAD

HAPPY
JOY
OPTIMISTIC

PEACEFUL
CALM
FOCUS

SAD
LONELY
UPSET

CONFIDENT
BRAVE
ACCEPTED

LOVE
APPRECIATED
CARING

ANXIOUS
WORRIED
SCARED

📖 Read until: "Sometimes the SPOTS have a hard time saying how they FEEL, so you may see them express their EMOTIONS in scribble ART, too!" Have you had a difficult time describing how you are FEELING? Have you created art to help you express yourself?

📖 Read until: "Scribble SPOT! You are not tangled anymore! See, don't you FEEL so much better?" Let's compare how Scribble SPOT looked before (tangled) with how he looks now (rainbow). How are they different and how do they make you FEEL differently? Tangled can make you FEEL confused, rainbow can make you feel happy.

✏️📺✂️ Rainbow SPOT Activity:

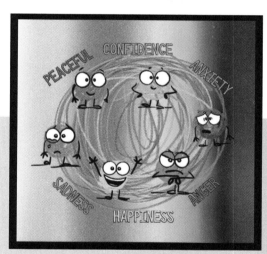

Appendix 186

Today, you will design your very own Scribble SPOT! Give each student a worksheet with two circles (to help younger students, you can provide a bullseye for the rainbow scribble.) One will be Scribble SPOT tangled, and the other will be Scribble SPOT rainbow.

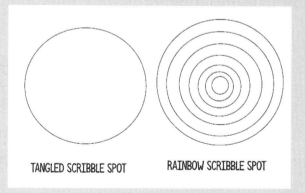

TANGLED SCRIBBLE SPOT   RAINBOW SCRIBBLE SPOT

Appendix 107

Show the students the sticker sheets. Now, we get to use these stickers to make EMOTIONAL scribbles! Which stickers would you use to show how your Scribble is FEELING?
○ Index cards work great.

Let's talk about colors and how they show FEELINGS and EMOTIONS. Which color should I use if I want to show that my Scribble is SAD? Go through each EMOTION: SAD, ANGRY, HAPPY, etc. (talk about what each one means) and have the students add that color to their Scribble SPOT!

 3-D Tangled Activity:

Materials Needed:
○ Either Wikki Stix, yarn, pipe cleaners, and/or Model Magic.

Take several colors and shape them into a ball, add stickers.

Melted Scribble SPOT Crayon Activity

Materials Needed:

○ Muffin tin and broken crayons

Step one: Have the students pick out various colors of crayons, take off their wrappers and break them. Coat muffin tin with baking oil. Place them into the muffin tin, ask the students what color this represents and name a FEELING associated with that color. Do you have a lot of FEELINGS inside you?

Step two: Bake the muffin tin at 270 degrees for 7 minutes. Once it starts melting, it goes pretty fast, so keep an eye on it. Pull the baking tin out of the oven, tap it a bit to level it. Then leave it out to cool -- you can also put them in the refrigerator. Once they are cool, tap the baking tin, and they will fall right out. Add scribble stickers for some fun effects!

Fine Motor Skills Center

○ Peeling the wrappers off broken crayons
○ Peeling stickers off a sticker sheet

FACIAL EXPRESSIONS AND BODY LANGUAGE

 Learning Objective:

Students will learn:

○ How to identify facial expressions in themselves and in others.
○ How to recognize and express FEELINGS.

What are facial expressions? Facial expressions are made using the muscles in the face that express a FEELING or EMOTION. They are a great way to communicate FEELINGS without saying a word!

What is body language? Body language is a way to express FEELINGS by the way we move our bodies.

Before reading:

Place some of the Jumbo FEELING and EMOTION flashcards around the room.

 Reading:

A Little SPOT of FEELINGS: EMOTION Detective
Introduce the book to the students.

This book will help you learn about FACIAL EXPRESSIONS and BODY LANGUAGE. Make a SAD face and ask the students, Can you tell how I'm feeling from my facial expression? Now cross your arms and make an ANGRY face. Let the students think for a few moments, then have them share some ideas with the class.

Do you remember seeing Scribble SPOT in another book I read? As I read this book, we'll think and talk about how Scribble is able to SEE FEELINGS by looking for CLUES.

 Read until: "Now use these clues to SPOT your FEELING and NAME IT! Once you name it, the final step is to SAY it and explain why! Start with I Feel.... when." A good example could be, "I feel frustrated when I struggle with something new." Now I want you to make hand binoculars to look around the room for facial expressions. Once the students SPOT a FEELING card, have them raise their hand and say, "SPOT FEELS...when."

After Reading: Use the flashcards and a mirror. Ask the students to make a similar facial expression and body movement that would be associated.

Closure:
Throughout the year, we will practice facial expressions and use words to explain how we feel. This will help us get along and communicate better with others.

Learning Objective:

○ Students will learn how FEELINGS and EMOTIONS are connected.

Introduction:

Today we are going to talk about the difference between FEELINGS and EMOTIONS and how they are connected. We all experience A LOT of FEELINGS, but there are only a few EMOTIONS. FEELINGS can either be the REACTIONS to an EMOTION or FEELINGS can CAUSE an EMOTION. It's important to know the difference. If you feel frustrated, it's good to recognize that FEELING and manage it before it becomes ANGER.

Playdough Activity:

Materials Needed:

○ Different colors of Playdough

Step 1: Create little balls of one color of Playdough. Explain to the class how these little balls represent FEELINGS.

Step 2: Then take all the little balls and mush them together to make one big ball. If your FEELINGS start to get out of control, they become one BIG ball of EMOTION.

 Bucket Activity:

Materials Needed:

○ Flashcards, seven buckets, or small boxes/bins

Step 1: From the deck of cards, pull out the EMOTIONS: ANGER, HAPPINESS, PEACEFUL, SADNESS, CONFIDENCE, LOVE, and ANXIETY.

Step 2: Place one card in front of each bucket.

Step 3: Pass out the remaining cards to the class. Then ask each student to come up and put their flashcard in the right bucket.

○ As another option: Use the plushies to identify the buckets.

 Discussion:

Has there ever been a time where your FEELINGS were getting out of control?

What could you do to help control those FEELINGS before they became a BIG EMOTION?

Let's think of some positive thoughts or FEELINGS to help us feel a BIG POSITIVE EMOTION!

FEELINGS Book Activity:

 ### Reflective Writing:

Reflective writing not only helps students develop self-awareness but also helps them with social awareness. Each of you will be creating a FEELINGS Book, and you will add to it each time we learn about another EMOTION or FEELING. This encourages the students to think about their thoughts, FEELINGS, and experiences.

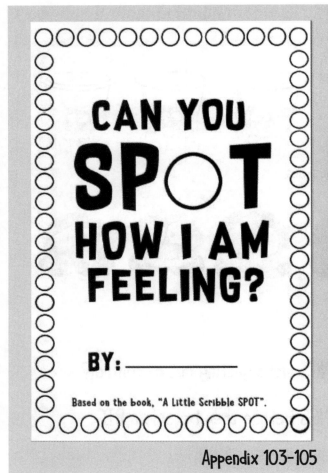

Appendix 103-105

EMOTION & FEELING Puppets:

To develop self-awareness, you need to identify your own EMOTIONS. It's also important to be able to link those FEELINGS with thoughts. Have the students color and cut out the EMOTIONS and glue them to Popsicle sticks (Appendix 100-102). Then ask the students to answer these questions by holding up the EMOTION:

Describe a time when you felt happy?
Describe a time when you felt sad?
Describe a time when you felt frustrated?

How do you feel when you can't do something you want to do? Why?
How do you feel when you see a large bug? Why?
How do you feel when someone yells at you? Why?

Appendix 100-102

 Discussion:

If students are answering the same question with conflicting emotions, for example: both ANGER and SAD, or both HAPPY and CONFIDENT, discuss how EMOTIONS can have different FEELINGS. Everyone can experience a situation differently, which would cause you to FEEL differently as well.

Additional Activities

Have the students create their own puppet faces. Observe if they understand how colors can relate to FEELINGS and EMOTIONS. Have the students play with their puppets and encourage them to show how the SPOTS help each other.

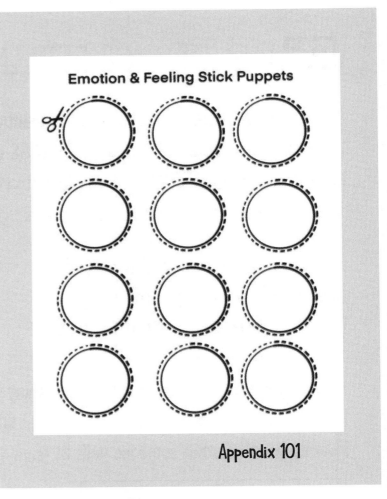

Emotion & Feeling Stick Puppets

Appendix 101

🗨️ Discussion:

To develop social awareness, you need to look at other perspectives. I want you to imagine how someone else FEELS when something happens. Putting yourself in someone else's shoes is the first step in learning EMPATHY. Dramatic play and role-play are where students begin to learn executive function skills. The students can act out the scenarios.

Anna spilled paint all over her drawing. How does she feel?
Jack forgot to bring his show and tell item to school. How does he feel?
It's Ryan's birthday, and he is getting ready for his party. How does he feel?
Jill's team won the game. How do you think she feels?
Joe received a thank you letter. How do you think he feels?
Mary lost her favorite toy. How do you think she feels?

Appendix 134-135 ✋

BIG EMOTION
COACHING

1 **Acknowledge the Emotion**
Let the child know that you see they are experiencing an emotion.

SAY
I can see something is bothering you...

2 **Label the Emotion**
Help the child understand what emotion they may be feeling.

SAY
Are you frustrated?
or
Are you feeling sad?

3 **Validate the Emotion**
All emotions are valid even if the emotion doesn't fit the problem.

SAY
It sounds like you feel_____ because of _____. Does that sound right?

4 **Problem Solve**
Help the child explore the problem.

SAY
Tell me what happened to make you feel this way?
or Let's look at some choices you have...

5 **Meet the Need**
Help the child move through the emotion

SAY
ANGER: I'm going to wait over here until you are ready.

ANXIETY: You're safe, I'm here for you. Tell me about it.

SADNESS: It's okay to cry, do you want a hug?

SADNESS: Needs Comfort ANGER: Needs Patience
ANXIETY: Needs Security

BIG EMOTION
FLOW CHART FOR KIDS

1 Emotion Check in
Acknowledge the Emotion

THINK
How am I feeling?

2 Label the Emotion
Try to put a word to how you are feeling.

THINK
Am I frustrated?
or
Am I feeling sad?

3 Validate the Emotion
All emotions are valid even if the emotion doesn't fit the problem.

THINK
I could be feeling_____
because of _____.

4 Problem Solve
What choices do you have?

THINK
If I took a break I could come back to this project when I'm not as frustrated.

5 Meet the Need
How can you help yourself move through the emotion?

THINK
ANGER: I'm going to take deep breaths, to find my PEACEFUL spot.

ANXIETY: I am going to remind myself that I am safe, and take a second to breathe.

SADNESS: It's okay to be sad, but I should find a loved one to talk to and get comfort.

SADNESS: Needs Comfort ANGER: Needs Patience
ANXIETY: Needs Security

✏️🖼️✂️ Jumbo EMOTIONS:

Cut out these jumbo faces and glue them to giant paper circles for an amazing display! Use color paper plates and paint stir sticks for a large puppet!

JUMBO EMOTION FACES

Appendix 168-175

○ Bulletin Board Idea

Feelings are O.K.

It's what you DO with them that matters!

○ Paint on white paper plates instead to use in centers!

✂️ Jumbo FEELINGS:

Cut out these jumbo faces and make things in the classroom have FEELINGS! Show how a chair, a table, or a bookshelf could be FEELING!

JUMBO FEELINGS FACES

Appendix 176-184

✂️ FEELINGS GAME:

Roll TWO dice to decide what SPOT will be created! Write a story about what the SPOT is doing and how he is FEELING!

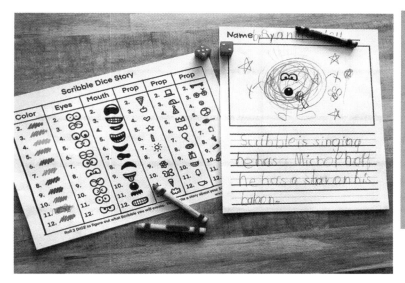

Color	Eyes	Mouth	Prop	Prop	Prop
2.	2.	2.	2.	2.	2.
3.	3.	3.	3.	3.	3.
4.	4.	4.	4.	4.	4.
5.	5.	5.	5.	5.	5.
6.	6.	6.	6.	6.	6.
7.	7.	7.	7.	7.	7.
8.	8.	8.	8.	8.	8.
9.	9.	9.	9.	9.	9.
10.	10.	10.	10.	10.	10.
11.	11.	11.	11.	11.	11.
12.	12.	12.	12.	12.	12.

www.diane.alber.com

Appendix 158-159

NOTES:

_____

_____

_____

_____

_____

_____

_____

_____

_____

_____

_____

_____

_____

_____

PART TWO: EMOTION EXPLORATION

- PEACEFUL SPOT
- SPOT OF ANGER
- SPOT OF ANXIETY
- SPOT OF SADNESS

- SPOT OF CONFIDENCE
- SPOT OF HAPPINESS
- SPOT OF LOVE

Self-management is the ability to manage one's thoughts, EMOTIONS, and behaviors in different situations to achieve goals.

TEACHING TIPS
- ○ Focus on building a classroom community.
- ○ Recognize students for their efforts in controlling EMOTIONS.
- ○ Be patient if a student is expressing a BIG EMOTION.
- ○ Help guide students through BIG EMOTIONS.

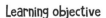
Learning objective

Educator Reading

Discussion

Hands-on: Arts and Crafts

Hands-on: Worksheets

Reminder: Areas presented in red text are intended to serve as the educator's script, if needed, for teaching the lesson.

PEACEFUL SPOT

Vocabulary:
EMOTION: PEACEFUL
FEELINGS: Relaxed, Calm, Focused, Serene

 Learning Objective:

Students will learn:

- Strategies to help stay calm.
- Self-management and the ability to manage BIG EMOTIONS.
- To identify when it's time to CALM down.

Name: _____

What PEACEFUL FEELINGS can you name?

Appendix 161

Students do not experience outbursts or tantrums because they want to. They do it because they lack the tools necessary to self-regulate. Students will identify stress-management strategies and will create a PEACEFUL SPOT either physically or mentally to CALM Down.

 Reading:

A Little PEACEFUL SPOT by Diane Alber.

Introduce the book to the students. This book will help teach us what to do when BIG EMOTIONS show up. We will learn how to calm down and focus. **Bring out the PEACEFUL SPOT plushie. Ask the class,** How does the plushie look PEACEFUL?

Do you remember when we read "A Little SPOT of FEELINGS: EMOTION Detective?" What are some PEACEFUL clues?

- Relaxed eyebrows
- Focused and learning
- Calm body
- Soft voice and breathing
- Ready to learn

Let the students think for a few moments, then have them share what they remember about the story with the class.

📖 **Read until:** "Is it your ANGRY SPOT?"

Ask the class, When was a time your ANGRY SPOT showed up? Were you frustrated? How were you able to find your PEACEFUL SPOT?
Were you able to take a deep breath and take a break?
Were you able to realize when you were FEELING overwhelmed?

📖 **Read until:** "Is it your ANXIETY SPOT?"

Ask the class, When was a time your ANXIETY SPOT showed up? Did you feel WORRIED? How were you able to find your PEACEFUL SPOT? Were you able to talk to a teacher or a friend about your WORRY?

📖 **Read until:** "Is it your SADNESS SPOT?"

Ask the class, When was a time your SADNESS SPOT showed up? Did you feel lonely? How were you able to find your PEACEFUL SPOT?

📖 **Read until:** "Let's look at some times you were PEACEFUL! Let's add things to your PEACEFUL SPOT." What are some things you can add to a SPOT in your room or the classroom to make it a "calming corner?" Would there be crayons? A giant pillow? Soft music? Fidget spinner? Toys?

CREATING YOUR PEACEFUL SPOT

PEACEFUL SPOT vs. Time out

We aren't born to learn how to self-regulate. Learning HOW takes time and effort. Time outs can be considered punishment to children, and BIG EMOTIONS can continue to linger after the time out is over. A PEACEFUL SPOT (calming corner) promotes a PEACEFUL place where children can calm themselves down. Children are not fully able to "think about what they have done" until they become teenagers, so this allows them to regulate their EMOTIONS instead.

Portable PEACEFUL SPOT:
- A comfortable and quiet place with EMOTION and FEELING flashcards.

Basic PEACEFUL SPOT:
- Print out FEELINGS posters and calm down signs, and provide a comfortable and quiet place to sit.

Interactive PEACEFUL SPOT:
- Everything a Basic PEACEFUL SPOT is, plus...
- Fill the room with sensory objects for example, a fuzzy rug, sensory toys and bottles, a cozy pillow, a small toy, a few stuffed animals.
- Have calming music and a place to color with crayons or markers.

"A Little CALM SPOT" by Diane Alber is an excellent book to read to help students learn how to do yoga and meditate.

Posters on Appendix 115-120, 185-186, 108-109

Sensory Bottle Activity:

Materials needed:

- Empty water bottle (Voss bottle)
- Vegetable oil
- Food coloring
- Trinkets, beads, buttons, dry goods, glitter, small items

Instructions:

Mix 2/3 vegetable oil and 1/3 water and trinkets inside the bottle using a funnel. Glue the top (lava lamp effect).

You can also just use water.

TEACHING PEACEFUL SPOT PROCEDURES

Key Points:
- How to use the PEACEFUL SPOT.
- What to do in the PEACEFUL SPOT.
- How to use different CALMING techniques/strategies.
- How to know when you can return to the group.

Going to the PEACEFUL SPOT:
- Explain the purpose of going to a PEACEFUL SPOT. It is a place for students to be able to CALM themselves DOWN.
- It can be used when an educator notices challenging behavior or conflict, but it is not used as punishment.
- The goal is for the students to use the corner independently and regularly and not as a punishment.
- Explain the importance of quietly going to the PEACEFUL SPOT (so they can respect their fellow classmates). Have the students practice.

- Students can also use a "Calm Corner Ticket" as a visual alert instead of a verbal call out.

Appendix 121

How to use a PEACEFUL SPOT:

- Practice identifying what FEELING caused you to enter the PEACEFUL SPOT.
- Explain that to get back to CALM and READY TO LEARN, it's helpful to use a calming strategy.
- If you are CALM and READY TO LEARN, you can return to the group.

Using Calming Techniques:

- Reference A Little PEACEFUL SPOT: What strategies did he teach us to find our PEACEFUL SPOT?
- Practice breathing techniques with the class.
- Ask the students if the PEACEFUL SPOT makes their FEELINGS more manageable. Why or why not?

Are You Ready to Return?

- Students need to identify when they are ready to return.
- Ask them how big their EMOTIONS are (ANGER, SADNESS, ANXIETY).

Rejoining the Group:

- It's essential to return the group the same way you entered, quietly and calmly.
- If a glitter sensory bottle is available, give it a good shake, and wait until all the glitter settles. This can help a student know when to rejoin the group!

Notes: Explain to the student that when someone is in the PEACEFUL SPOT they should keep working and give them space. Do NOT stare or giggle at them. The PEACEFUL SPOT is where a student can go to get focused.

Read until: "Let's add a chart for CALM Breathing too!"

Talk about Patterns and how breathing can be like a pattern! Draw a pattern on the board that resembles the dots and swirls in the book. Now have the entire class breathe in and out with the pattern.

After Book Activities

Have the students create their breathing SPOT pattern chart using different types of lines!

Appendix 117

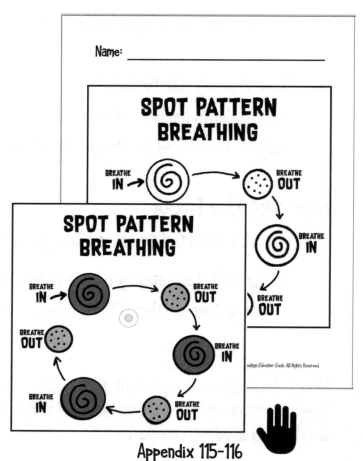

Appendix 115-116

 Breathing Circle:

Material Needed:

● Two different color paper plates and a black marker

Have the class sit in a circle, give each student a paper plate and a marker to create a pattern of swirls and dots. Then have the students take turns holding up their plate. Explain that every time they see a swirl, they breathe in, and dots they breathe out!

FEELINGS Book:

This will be the first page in their FEELINGS book! Have them decorate the cover and draw and write about a time when they were PEACEFUL and CALM.

I feel CALM when...

PEACEFUL when....

Appendix 105

PEACEFUL
CLUES ARE:

● Eyebrows relaxed.

● Eyes focused.

● Mouth calm.

● Soft voice.

● Arms relaxed.

SPOT OF ANGER

EMOTION: ANGER
FEELINGS: Frustrated, Mad, Jealous, Failure, Furious, Annoyed, Irritated

 Learning Objective:

Students will learn:

- How to identify frustrations related to situations/events (triggers).
- How people react differently to the same situation.
- How to express ANGER without hurting yourself or others.

 Reading:

A Little SPOT of ANGER by Diane Alber.
Introduce the book to the students. This book will help teach us about ANGER and how to manage it.

Read until: "It's okay to have small SPOTS of EMOTIONS, but when they get TOO big, it doesn't make you feel very good." Ask the students if they know how to shrink their ANGRY SPOT down to a PEACEFUL size? Talk about some of the strategies they learned from PEACEFUL SPOT. Have the students complete the ANGRY FEELINGS worksheet (page 151).

Name: _____

What ANGRY FEELINGS can you name?

Appendix 162

Read until: "I know of a special trick to get your ANGRY SPOT to calm down..." Ask the students to hold up their hand and show them how to count their SPOTS. Let's all say this together: Count your SPOTS from one to four. Tap, tap, tap and tap once more. Now fill your lungs with PEACEFUL air and coat your SPOTS with LOVE and care.

Read until: "Here is another situation where an ANGRY SPOT gets too big!" Explain to the students that these situations are also known as triggers, or things that "push your buttons." Can you think of a situation that pushed your buttons?

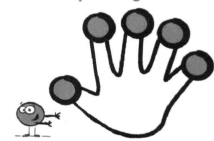

After Reading Activity:

Appendix 124-125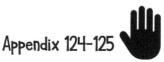

FEELINGS Book:

Have the students write and draw about a time when they felt ANGRY and FRUSTRATED....

Appendix 105

Pressing the RED Button:

Use the whiteboard and ask the students how ANGER makes them feel. Write down those FEELINGS on the board. Ask the students to complete the checklist. Place a large red button next to each feeling (you can also use red paper plates).

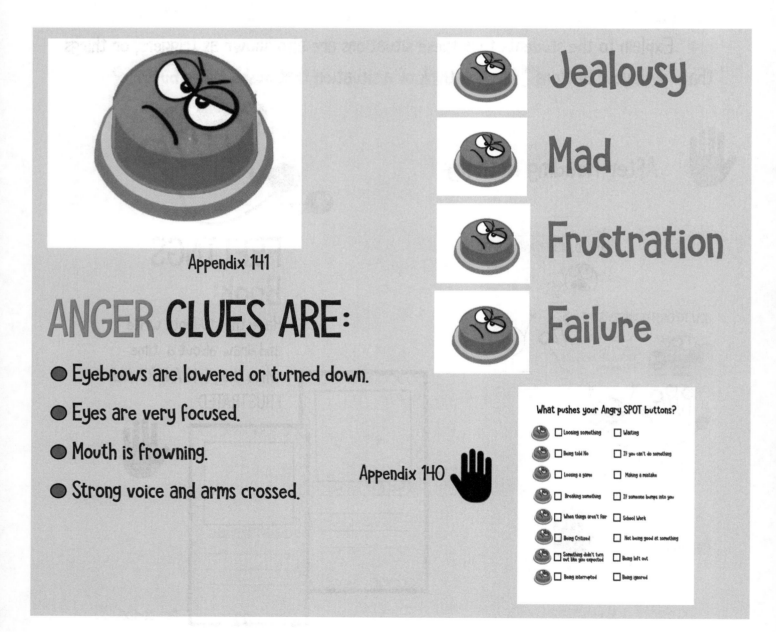

Appendix 141

ANGER CLUES ARE:

- Eyebrows are lowered or turned down.
- Eyes are very focused.
- Mouth is frowning.
- Strong voice and arms crossed.

Jealousy

Mad

Frustration

Failure

Appendix 140

What pushes your Angry SPOT buttons?

- ☐ Loosing something
- ☐ Being told No
- ☐ Loosing a game
- ☐ Breaking something
- ☐ When things aren't fair
- ☐ Being Critized
- ☐ Something didn't turn out like you expected
- ☐ Being interrupted

- ☐ Waiting
- ☐ If you can't do something
- ☐ Making a mistake
- ☐ If someone bumps into you
- ☐ School Work
- ☐ Not being good at something
- ☐ Being left out
- ☐ Being ignored

⚠ Beware of latex allergies in the classroom when using balloons.

 Balloon Activity:

Material needed: ● RED BALLOON

Now call on several students to come up to the board to push the ANGER FEELING BUTTONS. Every time a student pushes the button, the educator takes a big breath to blow up the balloon.

What will happen if I keep blowing up the balloon? **Every time the balloon is blown, continue to ask these questions:**

What happens if we keep pressing more ANGER Buttons? Will it explode? Pop? Fly around the room?

How is this like our ANGRY SPOT?

What is a safe way to shrink the balloon? Letting a little air out at a time. SLOWLY.

🗨 **Discussion:**

What are some ways to shrink our ANGRY SPOT? **Talk about the strategies in the book.**

Closure:

Remind the class that we all get upset and ANGRY sometimes. Point out from the push button worksheet, that we all get frustrated in different situations. We need to understand that we have the power to control our actions. We can all be kind.

Anxiety

EMOTION: ANXIETY
FEELINGS: Worried, Scared, Afraid, Anxious, Fearful, Concerned, Shy

 Learning Objective:

Students will learn:

- How WORRIES can become overwhelming.
- How to identify the difference between a GOOD WORRY and a SPINNING WORRY and how to CALM their ANXIETY.

Name: _____

What ANXIETY FEELINGS can you name?

Appendix 167

Materials needed:

- Backpack and several items (examples: one shoe, a rock, a pencil, etc.)

 Reading:

A Little SPOT of WORRY by Diane Alber.

Introduce the book to the students.
This book is going to help us understand our WORRIES a little more. As you read the book, focus heavily on the differences between a USEFUL WORRY and a SPINNING WORRY.

✋ Backpack Activity:

Before Activity:

The educator fills a backpack with USEFUL items, such as a ruler, pencil, and notebook. Now add in several large, heavy items that are not useful, such as a rock, a single shoe, and a stick.

During Activity:

Walk across the room with the backpack on and complain about how heavy it is. The stuff in my backpack makes it heavy and tiring to carry. It is hard for me to walk, dance, or have fun. What do you carry in your backpacks? What do you think I might have in mine?

Set the backpack on the ground and begin to remove the large, heavy USELESS items, saying, Wow, why did I pack so many USELESS things? These really made my backpack so heavy!"

Then pull out the USEFUL supplies, like pencils, notebook, markers etc., and say, I am glad I packed these USEFUL things. I need pencils and a notebook for school. **Place them back in the backpack.** Put it back on and be so excited about how lightweight it is and how easy it is to dance and have fun!

Point to the items you pulled out that were USELESS and heavy. These USELESS items are like your SPINNING WORRIES; you don't need them, and it makes it hard to have fun.

WORRY Box/Pocket Activity:

Learning Objective:

Students will learn:

- How to deal with WORRIES in a positive way.
- How to talk out their WORRIES.

Materials needed:

- Empty tissue box, shipping box, or use a paper box template that the students can decorate.

Read until: "Sometimes it can help to write or draw it out too and schedule a time with an adult to discuss them later. Just make sure you put them in a place where you will remember them. Like a box or your pocket!" You are going to make a WORRY box! Students will decorate and make their WORRY box. This gives them a sense of ownership of their WORRIES. Label the box WORRY BOX.

- When you send the WORRY box home, include a note to the parents explaining what it is used for.

1) Agree on a time the parent and child will check the box or add WORRIES to the box.

2) After the WORRY is discussed, spend a few moments to say something positive.

3) Discuss how you should get rid of the paper notes. Some children want to rip them up, stomp on them, or just give them to you so that they are not carrying the weight around with them anymore.

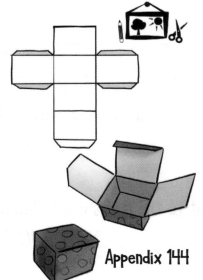

Appendix 144

● WORRY Pocket can be an alternative to a WORRY Box. The pocket can be taped to the back of the WORRY or ANXIETY book.

Appendix 145

I feel WORRIED when....

This box helps SPINNING WORRIES disappear, Just write or draw your note right here.

FEELINGS Book:

Have the students add another page to their FEELINGS Book. Have them write and draw a time when they felt WORRIED.

Appendix 105

 **Reading:**

A Little SPOT of ANXIETY by Diane Alber.

Show the cover to the class and see if they recognize the ANXIETY SPOT! Now refer back to A Little SPOT of WORRY and point how lots of little SPINNING WORRIES can become a BIG ANXIETY SPOT.

● Image from A Little SPOT of WORRY

ANXIETY CLUES ARE:

● Eyebrows are turned up and wrinkled.
● Head and eyes look down.
● Slouching and not smiling.
● Sweating and tummy ache.

 **Read until:** "Now imagine four gray SPOTS on your fingers and one green SPOT On your hand." Encourage the students to hold up their hands. Now repeat after me while making the hand motion.

From the tip of my finger
to the middle of my palm,
I can do this, I can be calm.
This WORRY grew too big and cannot stay,
take a deep breath and blow it away.

Name: _____

HOW TO CALM
YOUR **ANXIETY** SPOT

From the tip of my finger
to the middle of my palm,
I can do this!
I can be calm!

This worry grew too big, and cannot stay, take a deep breath and blow it away!

HOW
YOUR

to the middle of my palm,
I can do this!
I can be calm!

This worry grew too big, and cannot stay,
take a deep breath and blow it away!

Appendix 128-129

I feel ANXIETY when....
_____
_____
_____

Appendix 105

FEELINGS Book:
Have the students add another page to their FEELINGS Book. Have them write or draw a time when they felt ANXIETY.

SPOT OF SADNESS

Sadness

EMOTION: SADNESS

FEELINGS: Lonely, Left out, Disappointed, Upset, Hurt, Discouraged, Down, Defeated

 ## Learning Objective:

Students will learn:

- ● BIG EMOTIONS and how to identify them in themselves and in others.
- ● Coping techniques.
- ● What is empathy?

 ## Reading:

A Little SPOT of SADNESS by Diane Alber

Introduce the book to the students.

This book will help us recognize SADNESS in ourselves and other people to help provide comfort. **Bring out the SADNESS SPOT plushie. Ask the class,** Look at this little plushie, how does he look? Why do you think he's SAD?

Name: _____

What SAD FEELINGS can you name?

Appendix 164

Read until: "Crying is one way a SADNESS SPOT releases energy, which can help you feel better. It can also show you when a person is feeling down so you can help them." Who in this room has ever felt SAD? What would you do if you saw someone crying?

 Discussion:

What are some things you can do if YOU feel SAD?

- Cry and treat yourself with compassion.
- Breathe and find your PEACEFUL SPOT.
- Look at pictures if you miss someone.
- Talk to someone about how you FEEL.
- Hug or squeeze a stuffed animal.
- Draw or write how you FEEL.

Appendix 126-127

Closure: We will all FEEL SADNESS at some point during the year. Remember to talk to someone who cares about you when you are feeling SAD.

 FEELINGS Book:

Have the students add another page to their FEELINGS Book. Have them write and draw about a time when they felt SAD and LONELY.

SADNESS CLUES ARE:

- Eyebrows turned up.
- Watery eyes or crying.
- Mouth turned down.
- Hands covering the face.

Appendix 105

EMPATHY

💡 **Learning Objective:**
- Students will learn how someone might feel in a given situation.

Explain to the students that everyone can help a SADNESS SPOT, even if it isn't your own. When you see someone SAD, the KIND thing to do is show EMPATHY. Do you know what EMPATHY is? It means when you feel "WITH" someone. You can imagine standing in their shoes (not their actual shoes--that would be weird) and guess how they must be FEELING.

What are some things you can do if you see someone SAD?
Ask if they are okay or if they want to talk. Be a good friend.
Sometimes, EMPATHY means just sitting with them and not saying anything, but being ready to listen. Imagine what they must be going through. Give them a hug, and tell them how much you care about them.

 Discussion:

How can you be a good listener?
Why is listening important?
Why is it important to look at the person while they are talking?
What are some ways you can show you are listening?
- Eyes are watching
- Ears are listening
- Mouth is quiet

Some great listening games: Simon says, freeze dance, telephone.

Closure: Remind the class they can use their active listening skills every day!

 Heavy Heart Activity:

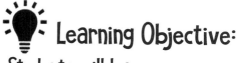 Learning Objective:

Students will learn:
- ● When to ask for help.
- ● How to identify when someone needs help.

Materials needed:
- ● Sponge & cup of water

(Optional: Cut the sponge in the shape of a heart)

Step one: Ask a student to hold the sponge. When this sponge is dry and light, it represents our hearts when we are happy.

Step two: Have the student place the sponge in the cup of water. Can you feel how heavy the sponge is now? This heaviness represents a SAD heart and the heaviness we feel along with SADNESS. People's words and actions toward one another can cause someone to be SAD.

Step three: Have the student hold up the sponge (water drips). These drips represent tears that we cry when we are SAD. Tears help move the SAD EMOTION out of our hearts. Humans are the only species that cry tears when they are sad. They help us move our SADNESS and make way for happy EMOTIONS.

Closure: Talk about the importance of having people around who care about them. It can be helpful to talk to these people, whether they are adults or friends. Let them know that all people, even grown-ups, need help sometimes. Being able to express SADNESS is very important because it lets people know that you might need help.

 Scribble Activity:

 Learning Objective:

Students will learn:

● How to identify different FEELINGS in different situations.

● How to include others.

Materials needed:

● I'm NOT just a Scribble... book

 Reading: I'm NOT just a Scribble.... by Diane Alber

This book will help teach us about including others. Can you remember a time when you were included and had fun? Can you remember a time when you weren't included? How did you FEEL? Let the students think for a few moments, then have them share some ideas with the class.

Discussion:

When have you felt confused?

Has anyone ever been mean to you?

Have you ever felt different and that you didn't belong?

Name: _____

What should the house have said to Scribble?
Draw your own scribble and write in what the House could have said to be kind.

Appendix 153

 Discussion:

When Scribble meets House, how do you think Scribble is FEELING?

How do you think House is FEELING?

Why do you think House is treating Scribble this way?

How do we know Scribble is SAD? **He's crying, he's looking down and blue.**

What does Scribble do to FEEL better? **He changes his colors.**

What have you done to feel better when you have FELT SAD?

Closure: Remind the students that no one wants to feel left out. When you choose to include others, you spread HAPPINESS.

 Power of Words-Toothpaste Activity:

Materials needed:

⬤ Toothpaste & Plate

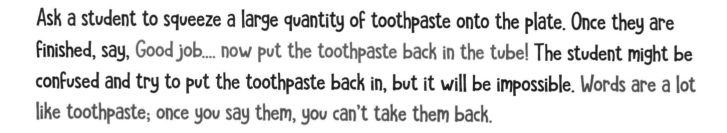

Ask a student to squeeze a large quantity of toothpaste onto the plate. Once they are finished, say, Good job.... now put the toothpaste back in the tube! The student might be confused and try to put the toothpaste back in, but it will be impossible. Words are a lot like toothpaste; once you say them, you can't take them back.

Closure: Point out to the students that just like putting the toothpaste back in the tube, it is very hard to take back hurtful words. We all need to be careful of what we say. Communicating thoughts and words is marvelous, but don't misuse that ability by speaking words that can hurt people.

BIG EMOTION REGULATION

 My Remote Control Activity:

Learning Objective:
○ Students will learn how to create a visual reminder that can help control BIG EMOTIONS.

Materials needed:
○ remote control worksheet

Introduction: This remote control allows us to remember some resetting steps to calm ourselves. This gives us time to decide how we want to react to a situation.

Appendix 142

Appendix 143

Step one: Show the students the worksheet. Remember that YOU are in control of your EMOTIONS and YOU have the power to bring yourself back to a calm place. This remote control is very important. It can help you change how you act and feel in a situation. You can CONTROL what you do and say to help manage your EMOTIONS.

Step two: Reflect on the books that have been read (ANGER, ANXIETY, SADNESS, and PEACEFUL) and point out how there are buttons on this remote control that help manage these EMOTIONS. There are even controller codes! Ask the students, What are some ways you can control ANGER, ANXIETY, SADNESS, and PEACEFUL?

Confidence

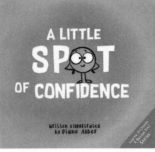

A LITTLE **SPOT** OF **CONFIDENCE**

Written & illustrated by Diane Alber

Vocabulary:

EMOTION: CONFIDENCE
FEELINGS: Accepted, Proud,
Determined, Brave, Valued

Learning Objective:

Students will learn:

● How to develop self-worth.
● Strategies and routines that can help build CONFIDENCE.

Reading:

A Little SPOT of CONFIDENCE by Diane Alber
Introduce the book to the students.

Name: _____

What CONFIDENT FEELINGS can you name?

Appendix 166

This book will help teach us how to GROW our CONFIDENCE. **Bring out the CONFIDENCE SPOT plushie.** Did you know this little CONFIDENCE SPOT likes to sit on your shoulder like this **(place CONFIDENCE on your shoulder)?** This way, it is close to your ear, and it can whisper positive thoughts.

📖 Read until: "In fact, I'm going to tell you a secret…Your family, friends, teachers, and guardians were helping you grow your CONFIDENCE SPOT even before you could remember." Ask the class, Can you describe a time someone made you feel special? Bring out the LOVE SPOT plushie too, and explain to the class different ways LOVE can grow your CONFIDENCE SPOT.

BELIEVE IN ME TREE Activity:

Name _____

BELIEVE IN ME TREE

Appendix 111

⬤ Paper plates can be used for a large display and the students can add notes to each plate!

📖 Read until: "Words are very powerful and they can change the way you see yourself." Can you say some positive words about yourself?

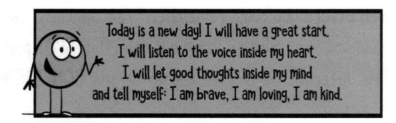

Today is a new day! I will have a great start.
I will listen to the voice inside my heart.
I will let good thoughts inside my mind
and tell myself: I am brave, I am loving, I am kind.

 Confident SPOT bracelets Activity:

Learning Objective:
💡 ● Students will learn self-worth and positive thinking.

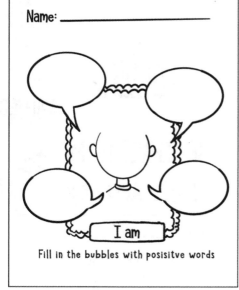

Name: _____

I am

Fill in the bubbles with posisitve words

Appendix 112

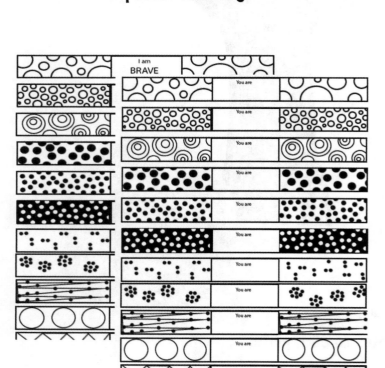

Appendix 113-114

Using the templates on Appendix 113 and 114, have students first design bracelets that reflect their FEELINGS of self-worth, with crayons and markers. Using the blank templates, each student designs a bracelet for a friend, filling it in with a positive word.

Learning Objective:

Students will learn:

- How being kind can help someone else build their CONFIDENCE.
- How to appreciate and accept uniqueness.

Reading:

Invisible Scribble by Diane Alber

This story is about a little scribble who doesn't feel like he fits in with the other scribbles.

Discussion:

What does the word invisible mean? **Can't be seen, or not noticed.**

What does the word discouraged mean? **Losing CONFIDENCE in your ability to be successful.**

Have you ever felt discouraged?

What is this story about? **This story is about a scribble that doesn't understand why he doesn't look like everyone else. He wants to feel important like the rest of the art on the wall.**

What challenges does Invisible Scribble face?

Why do the other scribbles help Invisible? **They help because they are kind.**

What event finally happens that helps Invisible feel included? **Scribble sees that it just takes time and effort to keep trying to find your purpose.**

What lesson does the author want us to learn? **You must try a lot of things to see what you are good at. Having caring friends who believe in you can help you feel confident.**

Including Others Chart Activity:

Show students the chart. Choose students to role play some of the scenarios that could happen in school. Have them come up with their own ideas for how to include others in activities.

Including Others		
Helping others feel VISIBLE (important) by including them		
Recess/Playground	Lunch	Classroom
Ask some one to play that is alone	Sit by someone new to make a new friend.	Say hello to someone new!
Invite kids to play with you.	Ask someone new to join your table.	Invite a new kid to join your work group.

Appendix 146-147

For example:

Recess- If you see someone sitting alone, ask them to play.

Lunch- If you see someone sitting alone at lunch, sit with them or invite them to sit with you.

Classroom- Invite kids to join your workgroup, say hi to someone you have not talked to before.

 Invisible Scribble Art Activity:

Materials needed:
- Paper, white crayons (not washable) and watercolor paints

Instructions:

Ask the students to scribble on white paper with a white crayon. Have them use watercolor paints on top of the white crayon. The wax will repel the paint, and they will start to see Invisible Scribble. After the paint has dried, they can decorate their Invisible Scribble with stickers.

Option Two:

Ask students to get into pairs. Have them create a secret note for each other using white crayons. Have the students swap notes and add the watercolor paint to them. As each student paints, they will reveal their partner's message.

Closure:

Remind the class we don't need to be like everybody else for people to like us. It's important for us to be able to recognize our own unique talents and individuality. We should be proud of who we are!

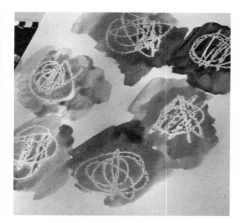

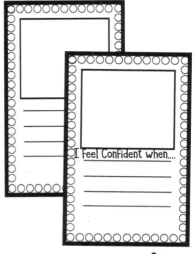

I feel Confident when....

Appendix 105

FEELINGS Book:

Have the students add another page to their FEELINGS Book. Have them write and draw a time when they felt CONFIDENT and ACCEPTED.

CONFIDENT CLUES ARE:

- Eyebrows are relaxed.
- Good eye contact.
- Mouth corners turned up and smiling.
- Strong voice.

Learning Objective:

Students will learn:

- How actions from others can build CONFIDENCE.
- How to build positivity in the classroom.

 ## Reading: Sticks by Diane Alber

Introduce the book to the students.

This book is about change. We can all help each other when someone is experiencing something difficult.

Materials Needed:

- Popsicle sticks, pencil, paintbrush stick

Before reading Sticks to the class, show the students a Popsicle stick, a pencil, and a paintbrush. Ask them what the items have in common and how they are different. They all have a different purpose; one is to hold up a Popsicle, one is to write, one is to paint. Do you think this stick knew it would be a Popsicle? It took a little help from the Popsicle stick factory for it to become a Popsicle.

These sticks represent everyone. We all need help from others to encourage us to believe in ourselves. We will experience challenges, struggles and mistakes along the way. If we can be a good friend and offer kind words, we can lift each other up. I'm going to read a story about a Popsicle stick who thought his only purpose was to be a Popsicle and when he melted, he felt lost. It took a good friend to help show him the way.

 Discussion:

What makes a good friend?

How do you make a friend?

What happened to Stick that he didn't expect? How did Twig help?

What what would have happened if Stick didn't have a friend?

 Popsicle Stick Activity:

Create the Popsicle before he melted

Material Needed:

- ⬤ Popsicle sticks, paper, crayons, glue, scissors

Name: _____

DESIGN YOUR OWN POPSICLE

Cut out the template, fold it and glue it on to a stick!

Appendix 139

Learning Objective:

Students will learn:

- How to build class community.
- The importance of motivation and determination in accomplishing goals.

 Discussion:

Hold up one stick. Can this stick alone build a birdhouse?

Now hold up two sticks. How about two sticks? Now, what if one stick was missing somewhere on the birdhouse? On the roof? Would it leak? Or how about the bottom? Would birdseed drop out? Everyone needs to be friends with others and support each other, even when someone makes a mistake or does something different than you do.

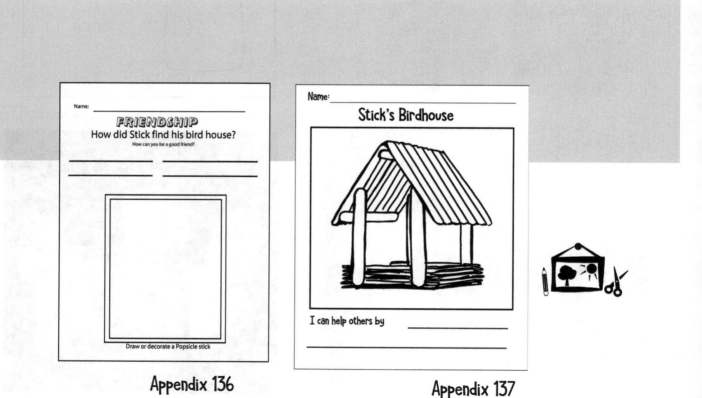

Name: _____

FRIENDSHIP
How did Stick find his bird house?
How can you be a good friend?

_____ _____

Draw or decorate a Popsicle stick

Appendix 136

Name: _____

Stick's Birdhouse

I can help others by _____

_____

Appendix 137

Bird House Activity:

Materials Needed:
- Jumbo craft sticks
- SPOTS stickers
- Hot glue (only to be used by an adult)
- Watercolor paint, acrylic paint or tempera paint or markers
- String (to hang the birdhouse)
- Clear acrylic sealer or polyurethane spray sealer

- Hand out the Popsicle sticks for the students to decorate. Have them write one positive word on each stick.

Instructions:

Step 1: Line up 8 jumbo craft sticks.

Step 2: Create a line of hot glue on top and bottom. Place a stick on both.

Step 3: Place two dots of glue on the ends and place a stick on top.

Step 4: Repeat to build the walls of the house.

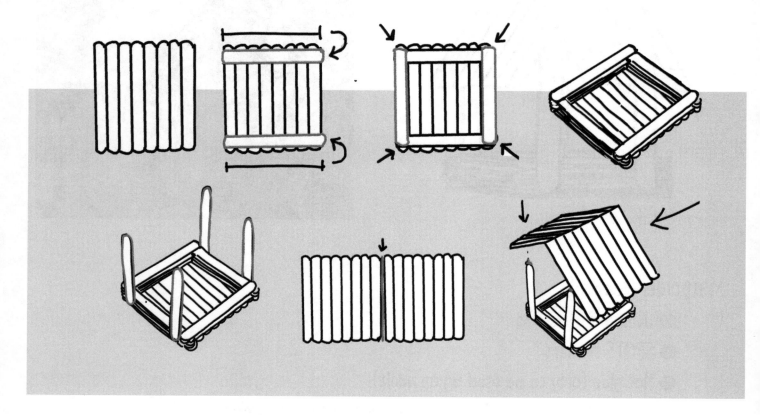

Step 5: Put hot glue on four sides to attach the posts.

Step 6: Do steps 1 and 2 to create two panels for the roof. Glue panels together at a 90-degree angle.

Step 7: Place hot glue on the posts to secure the roof.

Step 8: Place a string under the roof to hang it! Decorate with paint or markers!

Step 9: Place SPOT stickers on to decorate!

Step 10: Add a sealant to protect it from the weather.

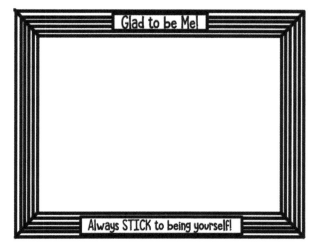

Glad to be Me!

Always STICK to being yourself!

Appendix 138

At the end of the story, Stick announced, "I'm glad to be me!" Can you decorate a Popsicle stick and add it to this frame?

Learning Objective:

Students will learn:

- How to accept differences.
- How to handle conflict in a positive way.
- It takes courage to stand up for what you think is right.

 Reading: Snippets by Diane Alber

Introduce the books to the students.

This book will help us understand that we are unique.

If we come together, our differences can make the world a better place!

Materials Needed:

- Color paper, scissors, worksheets

 Discussion:

Who lives in the paper place: What do they have in common? They all have equal sides and equal angles. They are called "regular polygons." Have the students create or draw additional regular polygons. Discuss what patterns are. The students can color this worksheet using a color pattern. Discuss the shapes in Snippet's shape pile: What do they have in common? They all have different side lengths and different angles. They are called "irregular polygons." Have the students create or draw some irregular polygons. Make a list and name them (right triangle, rectangle, parallelogram, trapezoid, kite).

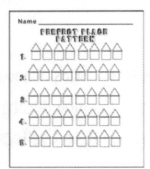

Appendix 152

Compare the two lists of polygons: How are they the same? They all have straight sides that connect. The sides don't intersect or have any spaces. They have at least three sides. This is the definition of a "polygon." How are they different? Regular polygons have equal sides and equal angles; irregular polygons don't.

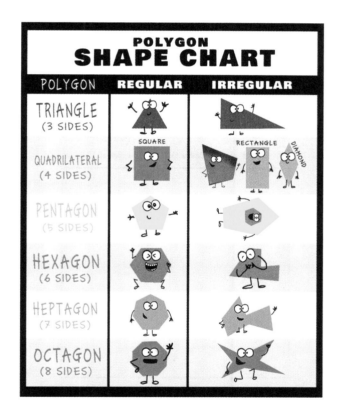

Appendix 148

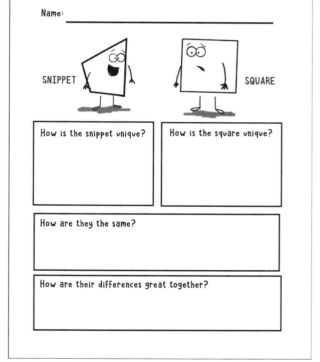

Appendix 150

Discussion:

How do Snippet's FEELINGS change as the book goes from beginning to end? What causes these changes? At the beginning of the book, Square just wanted things to stay the same; he is scared to try something new. Has this ever happened to you? When has trying something new ended up being a good thing for you?

Review the concept that people come in all shapes, sizes, and colors. No matter how we look on the outside, we all have FEELINGS inside us. Acting bossy or being treated unkindly keeps us from getting along.

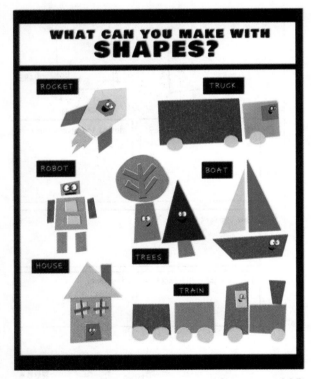

Appendix 149

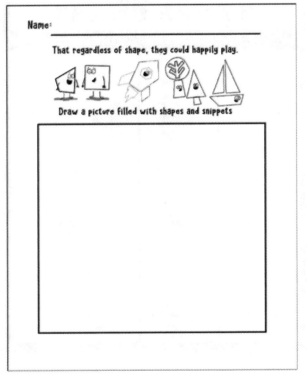

Appendix 151

 Discussion:

Have you ever wanted to be included but you were left out?

How did it make you FEEL?

Have you ever been teased about the way you looked?

It's not okay to tease people because they look different from you.

Closure: We are all different, and that is wonderful. Our classroom is a caring and kind place where we treat others with respect.

Snippet Craft Activity:

Use SPOT stickers faces and cut construction paper and glue the Snippets to a piece of paper to make a mosaic.

SPOT OF HAPPINESS

Happiness

A LITTLE
SPOT
OF **HAPPINESS**

written & illustrated
by Diane Alber

Vocabulary:
EMOTION: HAPPINESS
FEELINGS: Joy, Optimistic, Silly, Goofy, Hopeful

 Learning Objective:

Students will learn:

- ○ How to spread kindness and have a positive attitude.
- ○ Strategies and routines that can help build CONFIDENCE.

Name: _____
What HAPPY FEELINGS can you name?

Appendix 163

Reading:

A Little SPOT of CONFIDENCE by Diane Alber

Introduce the book to the students. This book will help teach us how to GROW our HAPPINESS. Bring out the HAPPINESS plushie. Ask the class, Did you know that one person has the power to grow hundreds of HAPPINESS SPOTS? What are some ways you can spread joy to others?

 **Link Activity:**

Materials Needed:

- ○ Construction paper

Every time someone does something kind, write it down and add a link.

HELPED A CLASSMATE
HELPED TEACHER
HELPED CLEAN UP

Tissue Box Activity:

Learning Objective:

○ Students will learn how they can help each other.

Materials Needed:

○ Box of pop-up tissues

Grab a tissue box with tissues. Watch what happens when I pull out a tissue. Do you see how the next tissue has already popped out? **Now pull another tissue out....**that tissue helped out this one!

The tissue that came out of the box HELPED pull the next tissue out! Then that tissue helps you dry your tears or blow your nose. When you help someone it brings them HAPPINESS.

Thankful Activity:

 ## Discussion:

Why is being thankful a great idea?
It can make us HAPPIER and shift our mood from bad to good.

Materials Needed:

○ An empty water bottle, shoelace, battery, & plastic container with a lid.

Introduce the items to the class. Explain why you are thankful for them
.

1) Water bottle: It's empty! I'm thankful that I was able to have a refreshing drink of water!

2) Shoelace: I'm thankful I had this shoelace to hold my shoe on when I went and walked my dog!

3) **Battery:** I'm thankful that this battery kept my flashlight on when the power went out.

4) **Container:** I'm thankful that this Tupperware was able to carry my lunch so I could have meatballs!

 ## Discussion:

We all have things in our bedrooms, living rooms, and kitchens that we could be thankful for, if we just stopped to think about them. When you go home today, I want you to look around and start writing about all the things you are thankful for. Here is a journal sheet to help! (Appendix 131)

 # SPOT Sticker Activity:
Learning Objective:
    ○ Students will learn different ways they can help each other.
Materials Needed: ○ SPOT Sticker DOTS, SPOT Sticker Chart

Hand out SPOT Stickers DOTS to the students. Explain that they will wear the SPOTS all day. At the end of the day, they will add their SPOT to the chart and share how they grew theirs or someone else's HAPPINESS SPOT. If a student can't think of anything, ask them what they are thankful for.

Appendix 130

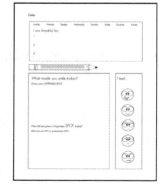

Appendix 131

A Little SPOT of KINDNESS by Diane Alber is a great companion to A Little SPOT of HAPPINESS. It includes scenarios of how students can be kind in everyday life.

 # Magic of Kindness (Magic Milk) Activity:

Materials Needed:

○ Milk, cotton swab, plate, Dawn dish soap

Instructions:

Step 1: Pour milk on the plate, completely covering the surface with a very thin layer of milk.

Step: 2: Place drops of food coloring in the milk. Explain that drops represent all of us and our FEELINGS.

Step 3: Put a small dab of Dawn on the end of the cotton swab. Explain that this cotton swab represents the smallest kind act. Ask the students to name some acts of kindness. Now have a student touch the center of one of a SPOTS with the cotton swab. As the color separates, explain that even the smallest act of kindness can make a big difference!

Science: When dish soap is dropped into milk, the soap molecules want to bond with fat molecules, so they swirl around trying to bond. The food coloring lets you see the process happening.

TEAMWORK

 Learning Objective:

Students will learn:

- ○ Teamwork and problem solving.
- ○ The importance of helping others.

 Reading: Scribble Stones

Introduce the book to the students.

This book is about how one kind act can change the world!

 Discussion:

When someone is kind to you it can make your day better. It makes us feel special and important.

Have you ever done anything to brighten someone's day?

How did Stone help Scribble and Splatter?

How did kindness travel all over the world?

Discuss different ways we can be helpful at home, in our neighborhoods, and at school.

 Scribble Stones Activity:

Today we are going to make Scribble Stones and place them around our school for people to find. What could we put on the stones to make someone smile?

Scribble Stone Art Project

Scribble stones are intended to inspire creativity and spread happiness through collaborative art.

HOW IT WORKS:

Find a stone and add some art,
a scribble, a splatter, or a happiness heart.
Then give it away and let someone know
that this scribble stone makes happiness grow.
It's so very simple and easy to do.
Just add some more art and give it away, too!

Give away   Give away   Give away

Appendix 132

 Scribble Stones Alternative:

If you don't have stones or would like an additional option, this worksheet can be found on Appendix 133.

Appendix 133

Closure:

Explain how we all have a HELPER inside of us, just like Scribble Stone. When we all work together, we can accomplish so much more.

Appendix 105

FEELINGS Book:

Have the students add two more pages in their FEELINGS Book. Have them write and draw about a time when they felt HAPPINESS and JOY.

HAPPINESS CLUES ARE:

○ Eyebrows raised.

○ Eyes are crinkling.

○ Mouth corners turned up and smiling.

SPOT OF LOVE

LOVE

Vocabulary:
EMOTION: LOVE
FEELINGS: Appreciated, Caring, Compassion, Special

 Learning Objective:

Students will learn:
- ● How to give and receive LOVE.
- ● How to identify LOVE and how they would LOVE to be LOVED.

Reading:

A Little SPOT of LOVE by Diane Alber
Introduce the book to the students. This book will help teach us how to GROW our LOVE in ourselves and other people, too! Bring out the LOVE plushie. Ask the class, Did you know that LOVE is full of a lot of FEELINGS? Bring out the PEACEFUL, HAPPINESS, and CONFIDENCE. plushie. What are some ways you think you can show LOVE?

Name: _____

What LOVE FEELINGS can you name?

Appendix 165

✋ Growing LOVE Activity:

Materials Needed:

⬤ SPOT Sticker DOTS from SPOT sticker book, three spray bottles, small potted plant, flower worksheet (Appendix page 155).

Step One: Place SPOT stickers on spray bottles and label them with HAPPINESS, CONFIDENCE, and PEACEFUL. Then place a PINK SPOT on the planter and label it LOVE. Discuss how these EMOTIONS can grow our LOVE SPOT.

Step Two: Have one student each day responsible for watering the plant with these EMOTIONS. Have the students measure the plant weekly to see how much it grows.

Step Three: Have the students write out on each petal how they want to be LOVED (examples would be hugs, being told "I LOVE you," being read to, etc.).

Appendix 155

Step Four (optional): Have the students cut out their flower. Then add leaves and stems from green construction paper and attach to a large board.

Name _____

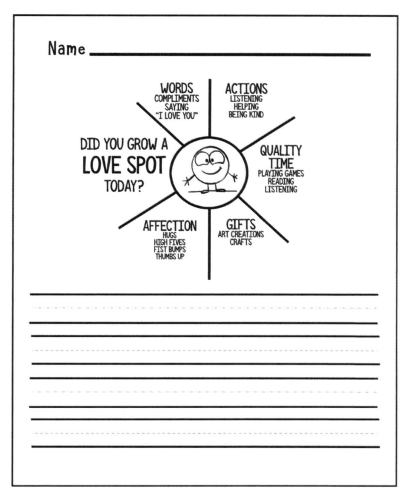

DID YOU GROW A **LOVE SPOT** TODAY?

WORDS
COMPLIMENTS
SAYING
"I LOVE YOU"

ACTIONS
LISTENING
HELPING
BEING KIND

QUALITY TIME
PLAYING GAMES
READING
LISTENING

AFFECTION
HUGS
HIGH FIVES
FIST BUMPS
THUMBS UP

GIFTS
ART CREATIONS
CRAFTS

● You can hang this poster up in your classroom and as the students walk in, they can choose how they want to be greeted!

HOW DO YOU LIKE TO BE GREETED?

High Five

Fist Bump

Wave

Thumbs Up

Appendix 154

Appendix 156

LOVE CLUES ARE:

● Eyebrows raised.
● Mouth turned upward smiling.
● Wrinkled eyes.
● Blushing and rosy cheeks.

I feel LOVE when___

Appendix 105

FEELINGS Book:

Have the students add another page to their FEELINGS Book. Have them write and draw about a time when they felt LOVE and APPRECIATION.

 # LOVE Snippet Collage Activity:

Materials Needed:
● Green, orange, yellow, and pink paper, glue, paper hearts and dot markers

Step One: Cut the colored paper into small and large snippets (students can do this or an educator can do it beforehand).

Step Two: Have the students glue snippets of paper on the heart, using different sizes of snippets.

Step Three:
While they are gluing, point out how the pieces are all different sizes. Sometimes it takes actions of all different sizes to grow LOVE SPOTS.

Another Option:
You can use different color dot markers on a white paper heart.

 Learning Objective:

Students will learn:

    ◉ Social awareness.

    ◉ How positive actions can have a chain reaction.

Materials Needed:

    ◉ Paper and jar

Reading:

Kindness Snippet Jar by Diane Alber

This story is about how kindness can brighten someone's day.

Read until: "Words are very powerful. Some words can make you happy, some can make you sad, and some can bring kindness! It's important to find the right words!" How do you feel when I say the words "You made me feel special?" These kind words can change someone's day for the better.

Read until: "I didn't find these words. I did something kind and they just appeared."

 Discussion: Do you know how to be kind?

Can you name some kind actions?

Kindness Snippet Jar Activity:

Here are two ways to use the Kindness Snippet Jar:

1) Every time a student is doing something kind, write it on a snippet and add it to the jar. Once the jar is full, everyone who contributed can receive a special reward.

2) Print kindness cards and place them in the jar. Have each student choose a card to prompt kindness throughout the day.

Appendix 122-123

NOTES:

_____

_____

_____

_____

_____

_____

_____

_____

_____

_____

_____

_____

_____

_____

_____

APPENDIX: ACTIVITY RESOURCES

This guide book refers to multiple printouts for you to use with the lessons. Make copies and use them with the students.

 ## TEACHING REMINDER

○ Get creative.

○ Try to give each student a few minutes of undivided attention.

○ There are valuable lessons that students can learn when working with groups. Use these opportunities to teach FEELINGS and how they respect FEELINGS of others.

99

Emotion & Feeling Stick Puppets

Emotion & Feeling Stick Puppets

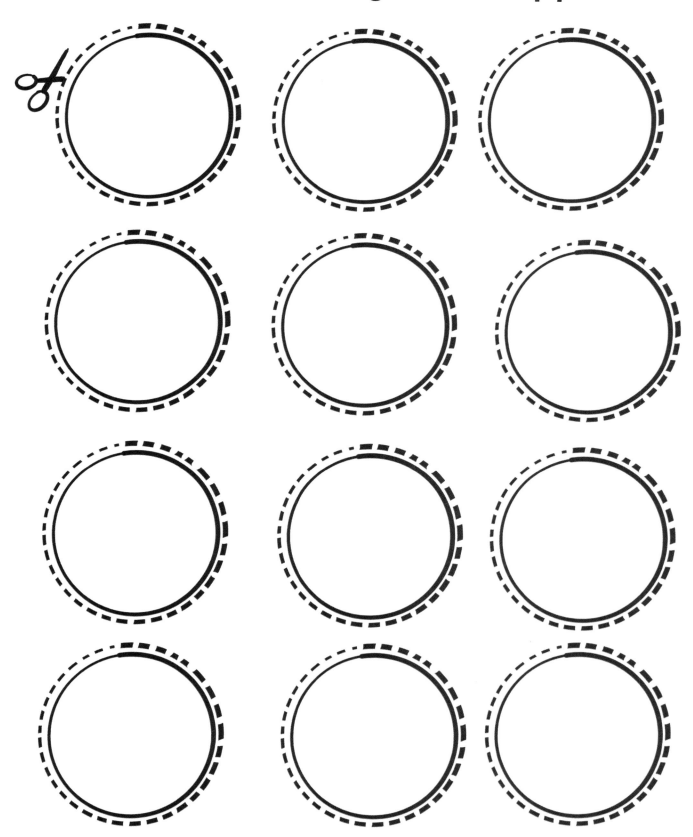

Emotion & Feeling Stick Puppets

CAN YOU SPOT HOW I AM FEELING?

BY: _____

Based on the book, "A Little Scribble SPOT".

Name _____

I feel _____ when...

_____
_____
_____
_____
_____
_____
_____

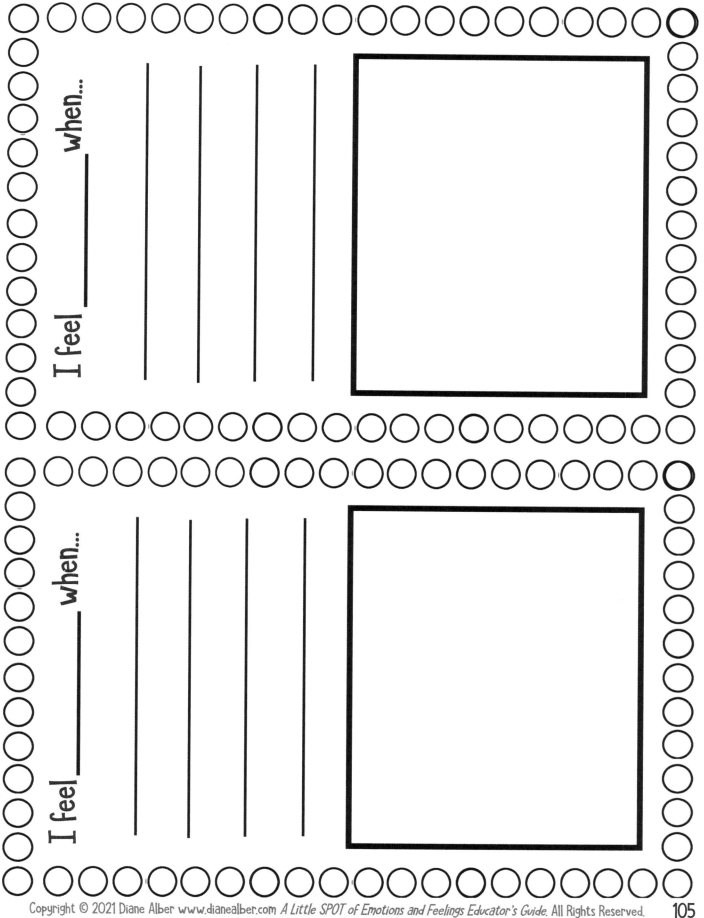

I feel _____ when...

I feel _____ when...

Name _____

Name: _____

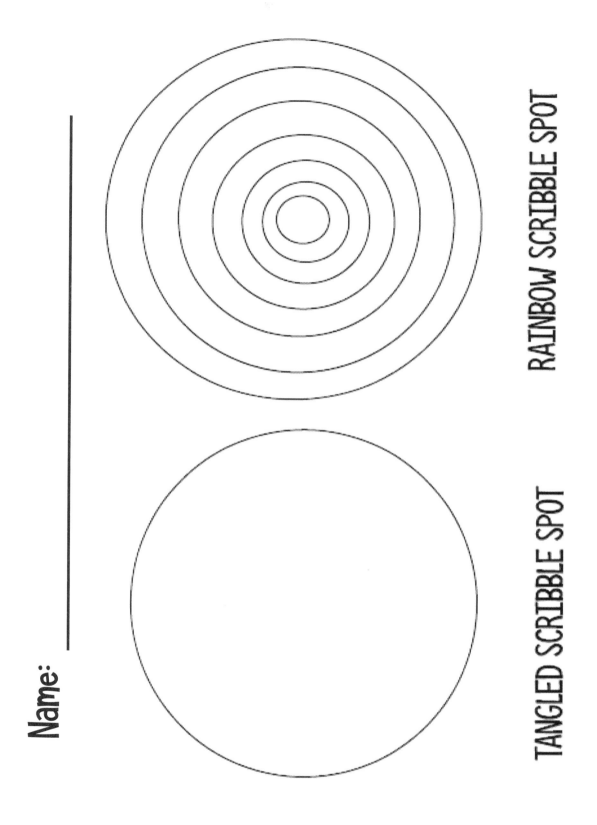

RAINBOW SCRIBBLE SPOT

TANGLED SCRIBBLE SPOT

HOW DO YOU FEEL?

 DETERMINED

 JOY

 OPTIMISTIC

 PEACEFUL

 HOPEFUL

 GREAT

 AT EASE

 ANGRY

 ANNOYED

 PROUD

 EXCITED

 SILLY

 CALM

 MAD

 IRRITATED

 BRAVE

 POSITIVE

 HAPPY

 RELAXED

 FRUSTRATED

 FURIOUS

 CONFIDENT

 GOOFY

 DELIGHTED

 CREATIVE

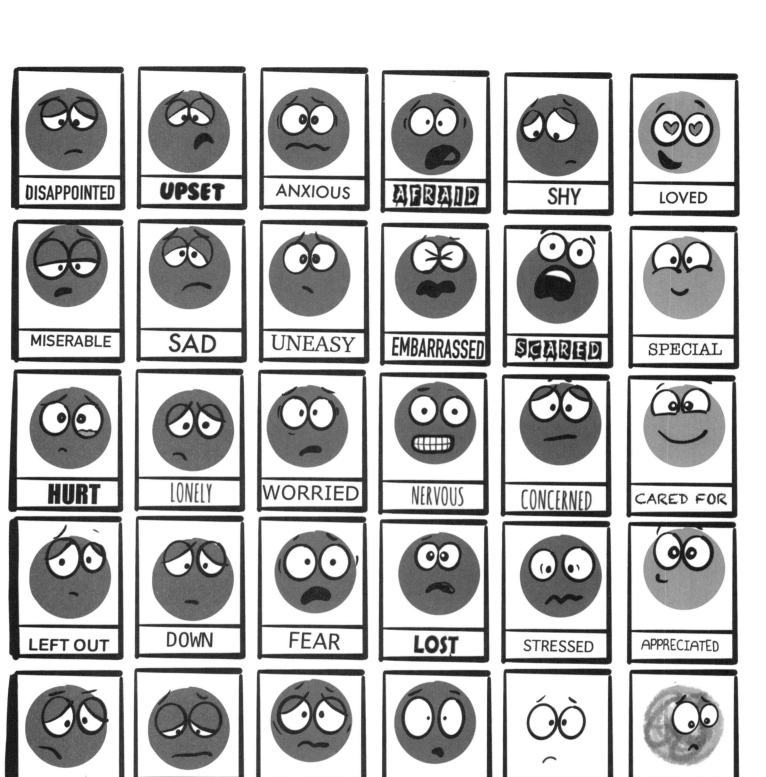

SPOT IT • NAME IT • SAY IT!
"I FEEL...WHEN....."

EMOTION CHECK-IN

1

2

3

4

5

Name _____

BELIEVE IN ME TREE

Name: _____

I am

I am
BRAVE

I am
LOVING

I am
KIND

I am
DETERMINED

I am
CARING

I am
LOVED

I am a good
FRIEND

I try my
BEST

I am
IMPORTANT

I am
PATIENT

I am a great
LISTENER

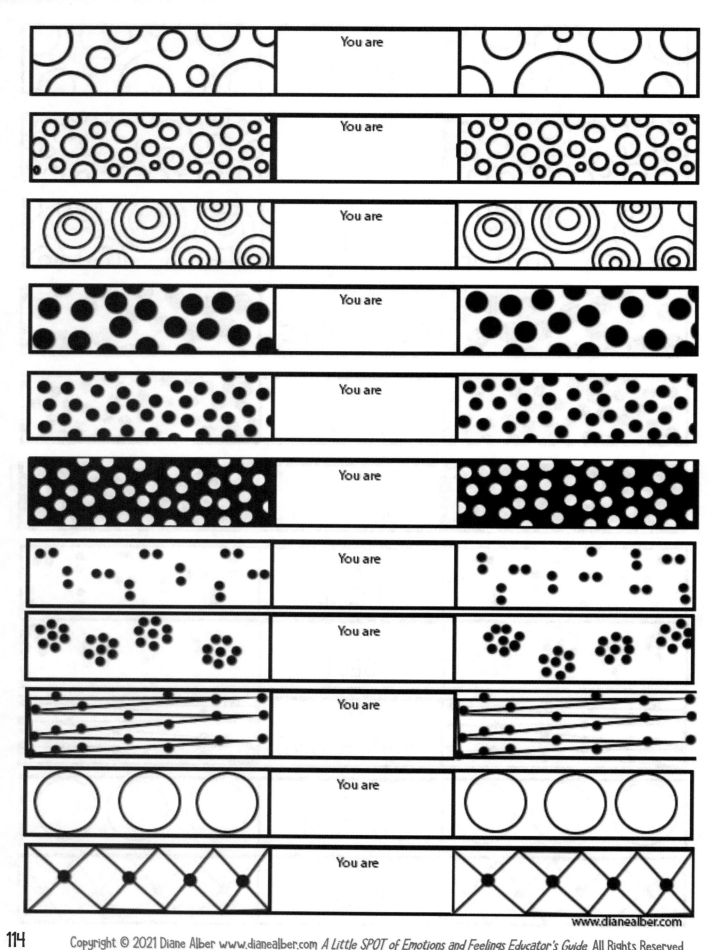

You are

You are

You are

You are

You are

You are

You are

You are

You are

You are

You are

SPOT PATTERN BREATHING

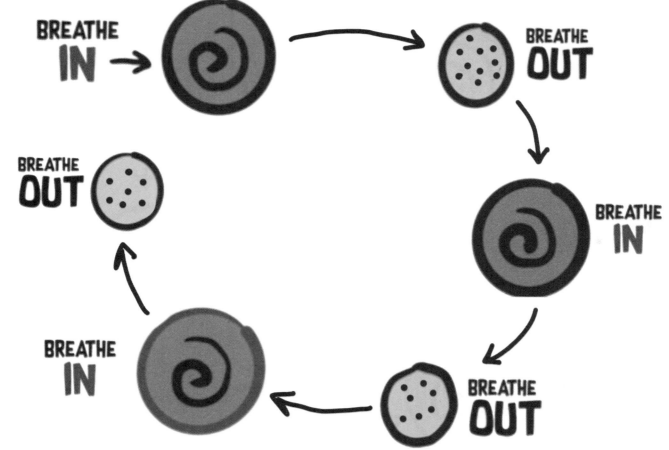

BREATHE **IN** →

BREATHE **OUT**

BREATHE **IN**

BREATHE **OUT**

BREATHE **IN**

BREATHE **OUT**

Name: _____

SPOT PATTERN BREATHING

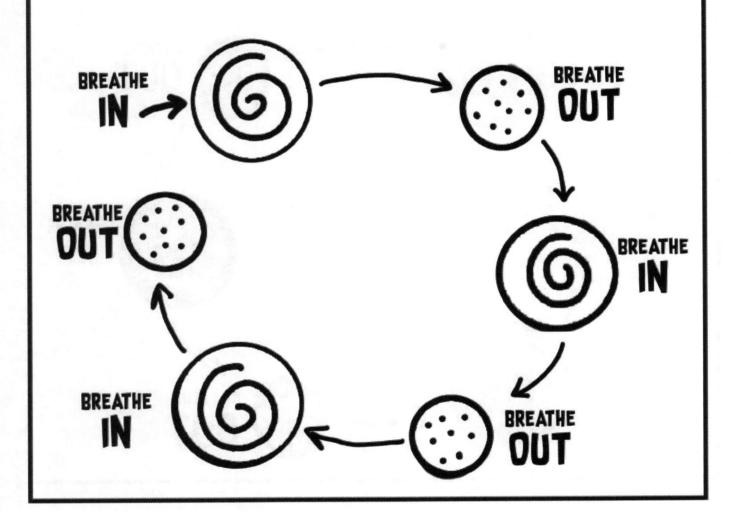

BREATHE IN

BREATHE OUT

BREATHE IN

BREATHE OUT

BREATHE IN

BREATHE OUT

Name _____

SPOT BREATHING

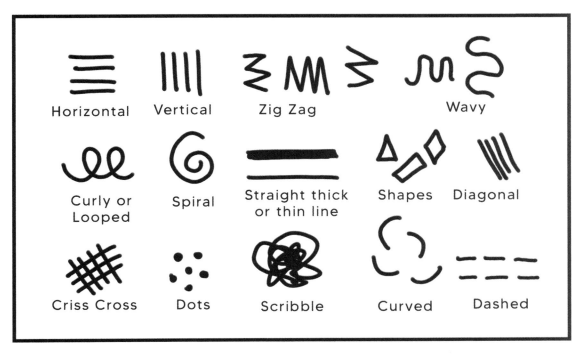

Horizontal   Vertical   Zig Zag   Wavy

Curly or Looped   Spiral   Straight thick or thin line   Shapes   Diagonal

Criss Cross   Dots   Scribble   Curved   Dashed

BREATHE IN   BREATHE OUT   BREATHE IN   BREATHE OUT   BREATHE IN   BREATHE OUT

BREATHING TRICKS

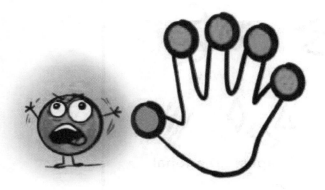

Count the SPOTS from one to four.
Tap, tap, tap and tap once more.
Now fill your lungs
with peaceful air,
and coat your spots
with love and care.

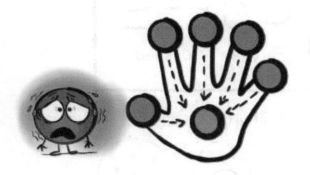

From the tip of my finger to the middle of my palm,
I can do this! I can be calm!
This worry grew too big and cannot stay,
take a deep breath and blow it away!

Circle the SPOTS in the middle of your palm,
count the swirls down to CALM.
Around and around, and around twice more.
One, then two, then three, then four.
Each time you trace around the SPOTS,
take a deep breath to CALM your thoughts.

SPOT YOUR FEELING

Nervous

Worried

Scared

Disappointed

Lonely

Loss

Annoyed

Hurt

Frustrated

Kindness Snippets

Kindness Snippets

MAKE SOMEONE SMILE ☺

BEFRIEND A LONELY PERSON

BE ENCOURAGING

Make ART for someone!

Give someone a compliment

Help someone

HELP CLEAN UP

Share something today

Smile at everyone you meet

Say please and thank you all day!

Be patient

Don't complain

Clean up after yourself

Make someone laugh

SAY SOMETHING NICE ABOUT SOMEONE

HOW TO CALM YOUR ANGRY SPOT

Count the SPOTS from one to four. TAP, TAP, TAP, and TAP once more.

Now fill your lungs with peaceful air, and coat your spots with love and care.

Name: _____

HOW TO CALM YOUR ANGRY SPOT

Count the SPOTS from one to four. TAP, TAP, TAP, and TAP once more.

Now fill your lungs with peaceful air, and coat your spots with love and care.

HOW TO CALM YOUR SADNESS SPOT

Circle the SPOTS in the middle of your palm,
count the swirls down to CALM.
Around and around, and around twice more.
One, then two, then three, then four.
Each time you trace around the SPOTS,
take a deep breath to CALM your thoughts.

Name: _____

HOW TO CALM YOUR SADNESS SPOT

Circle the SPOTS in the middle of your palm,
count the swirls down to CALM.
Around and around, and around twice more.
One, then two, then three, then four.
Each time you trace around the SPOTS,
take a deep breath to CALM your thoughts.

HOW TO CALM
YOUR ANXIETY SPOT

From the tip of my finger
to the middle of my palm,
I can do this!
I can be calm!

This worry grew too big, and cannot stay,
take a deep breath and blow it away!

Name: _____

HOW TO CALM
YOUR ANXIETY SPOT

From the tip of my finger to the middle of my palm,

I can do this!
I can be calm!

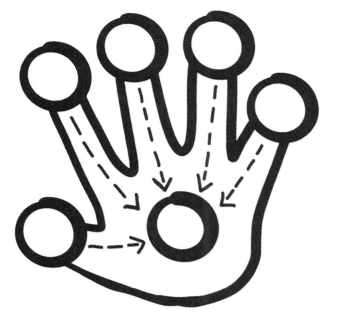

This worry grew too big, and cannot stay, take a deep breath and blow it away!

SPOT CARD

| Monday | Tuesday | Wednesday |

| Thursday | Friday | Saturday | Sunday |

How did you grow a HAPPINESS SPOT?

Mark a spot on every day you grow a HAPPINESS SPOT!
Can you spread HAPPINESS all week?

Date:

Sunday	Monday	Tuesday	Wednesday	Thursday	Friday	Saturday	Sunday

I am thankful for:

1.

2.

3.

What made you smile today?

Draw your HAPPINESS SPOT:

How did you grow a Happiness SPOT today?

(Either your own SPOT or someone else's SPOT.)

Scribble Stone Art Project

Scribble stones are intended to inspire creativity and spread happiness through collaborative art.

HOW IT WORKS:

Find a stone and add some art,
a scribble, a splatter, or a happiness heart.
Then give it away and let someone know
that this scribble stone makes happiness grow.
It's so very simple and easy to do.
Just add some more art and give it away, too!

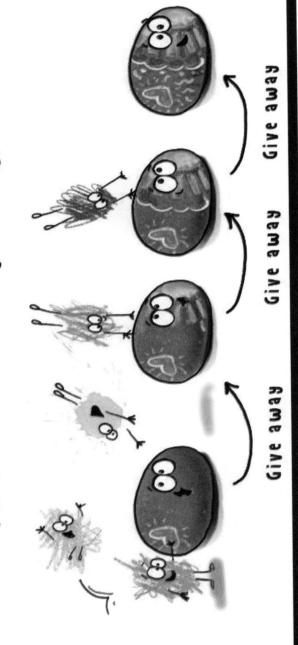

Give away   Give away   Give away   Give away

NAME _____

SCRIBBLE STONE

INSPIRATION:

WORDS

Kind Brave
Hope Love
Smile Joy
Dream Trust
Peace Forgive

DESIGN

//// ♡ ☆ ◎ ∴ MM ✳
ᵜᵜᵜ △ ▢ ○ ⧨ ⊓⊓⊓ ◎

FACES:

Name: _____

FRIENDSHIP
How did Stick find his bird house?
How can you be a good friend?

_____   _____

_____   _____

Draw or decorate a Popsicle stick

Name: _____

Stick's Birdhouse

I can help others by

_____

Name:

Glad to be Me!

Always STICK to being yourself!

Name:

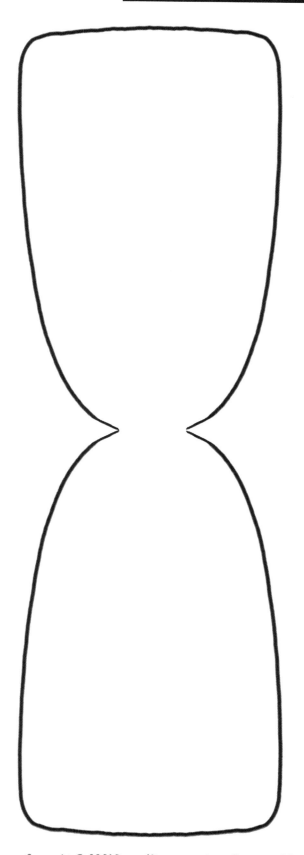

DESIGN YOUR OWN POPSICLE

Cut out the template, fold it and glue it on to a stick!

Name: _____

What pushes your Angry SPOT buttons?

☐ Losing something   ☐ Waiting

☐ Being told No   ☐ If you can't do something

☐ Losing a game   ☐ Making a mistake

☐ Breaking something   ☐ If someone bumps into you

☐ When things aren't fair   ☐ School work

☐ Being criticized   ☐ Not being good at something

☐ Something didn't turn out like you expected   ☐ Being left out

☐ Being interrupted   ☐ Being ignored

Name: _____

I AM IN CONTROL
OF MY EMOTIONS

IN CONTROL IS HOW I ROLL

Controller Codes

Press the Emotion you are feeling:

Press the say it button  and say why you are feeling that way.

Count   Breathe in and out twice   Peaceful thought

I AM IN CONTROL
OF MY EMOTIONS
IN CONTROL IS HOW I ROLL

I AM IN CONTROL

Controller Codes

Press the Emotion you are feeling:

Press the say it button and say why you are feeling that way.

Count   Breathe in and out twice   Peaceful thought

WORRY BOX

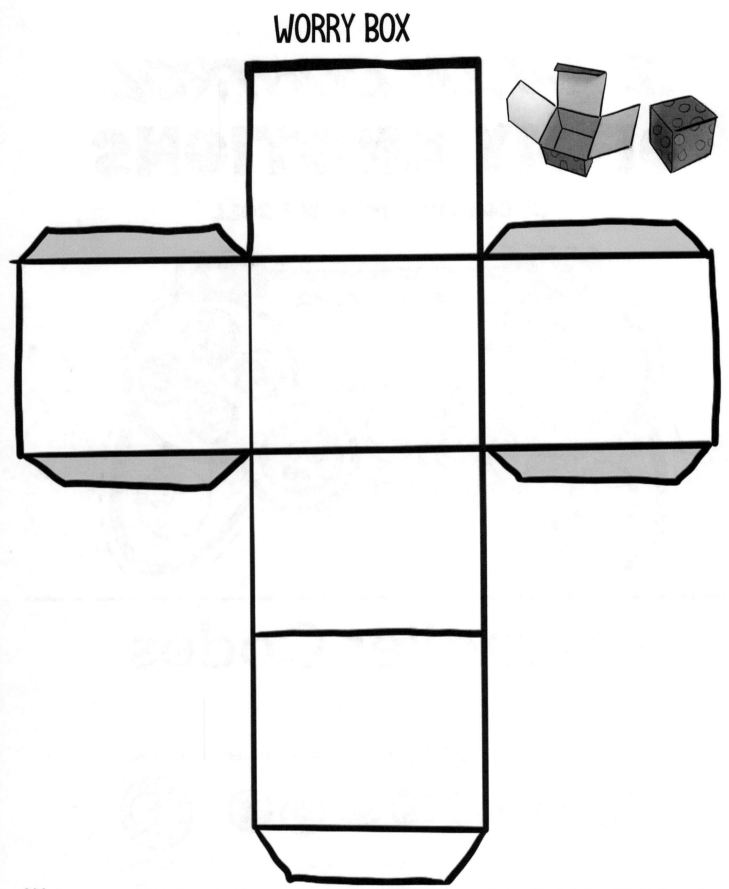

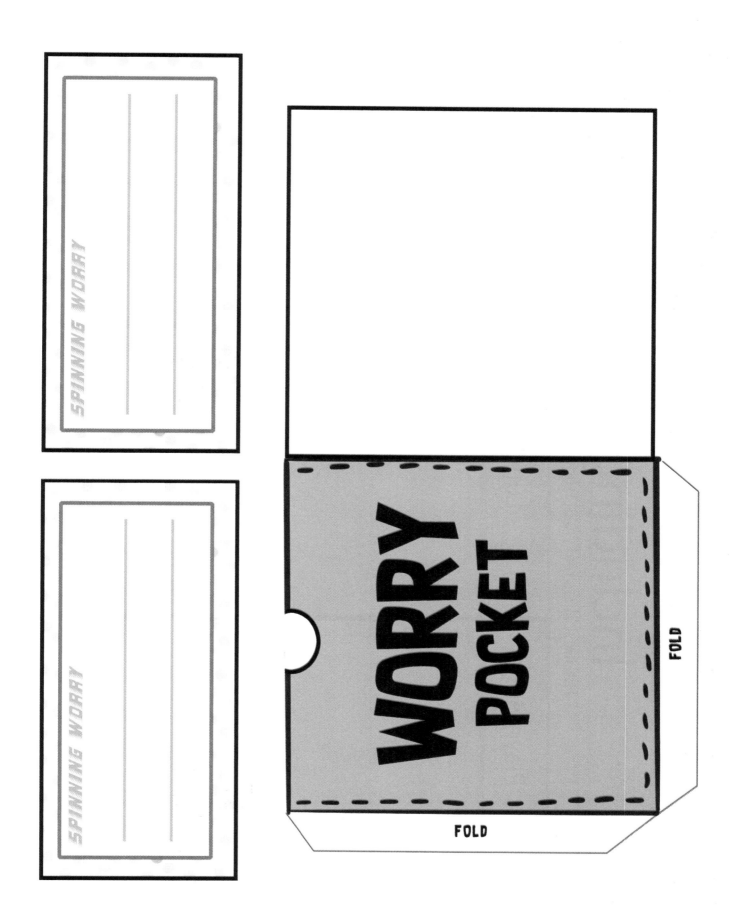

SPINNING WORRY

SPINNING WORRY

WORRY POCKET

FOLD

FOLD

Name: _____

Including Others

Helping others feel VISIBLE (important) by including them

Recess/Playground	Lunch	Classroom

Including Others

Helping others feel VISIBLE (important) by including them

Recess/Playground	Lunch	Classroom
Ask some one to play that is alone!

Invite kids to play with you. | Sit by someone new to make a new friend.

Ask someone new to join your table. | Say hello to someone new!

Invite a new kid to join your work group. |

POLYGON
SHAPE CHART

POLYGON	REGULAR	IRREGULAR
TRIANGLE (3 SIDES)		
QUADRILATERAL (4 SIDES)	SQUARE	RECTANGLE · DIAMOND
PENTAGON (5 SIDES)		
HEXAGON (6 SIDES)		
HEPTAGON (7 SIDES)		
OCTAGON (8 SIDES)		

WHAT CAN YOU MAKE WITH
SHAPES?

ROCKET

TRUCK

ROBOT

BOAT

TREES

HOUSE

TRAIN

Name: _____

SNIPPET

SQUARE

How is the snippet unique?

How is the square unique?

How are they the same?

How are their differences great together?

Name:

That regardless of shape, they could happily play.

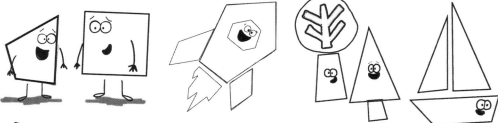

Draw a picture filled with shapes and snippets

Name _____

PERFECT PLACE PATTERN

1.

2.

3.

4.

5.

Name: _____

What should the house have said to Scribble?
Draw your own scribble and write in what the House could have said to be kind.

Name _____

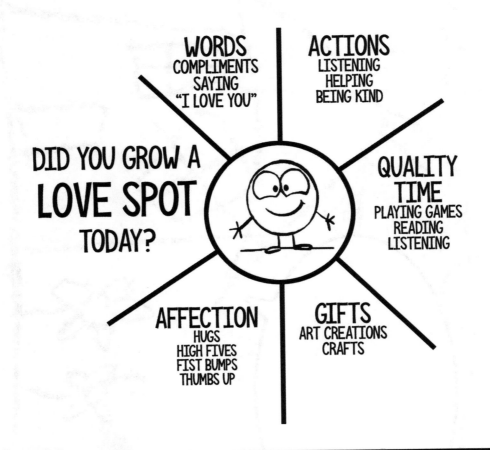

WORDS
COMPLIMENTS
SAYING
"I LOVE YOU"

ACTIONS
LISTENING
HELPING
BEING KIND

DID YOU GROW A
LOVE SPOT
TODAY?

QUALITY
TIME
PLAYING GAMES
READING
LISTENING

AFFECTION
HUGS
HIGH FIVES
FIST BUMPS
THUMBS UP

GIFTS
ART CREATIONS
CRAFTS

Name: _____

Growing LOVE

How I want to be LOVED...

HOW DO YOU LIKE TO BE GREETED?

Name: _____

Create your own SPOT!

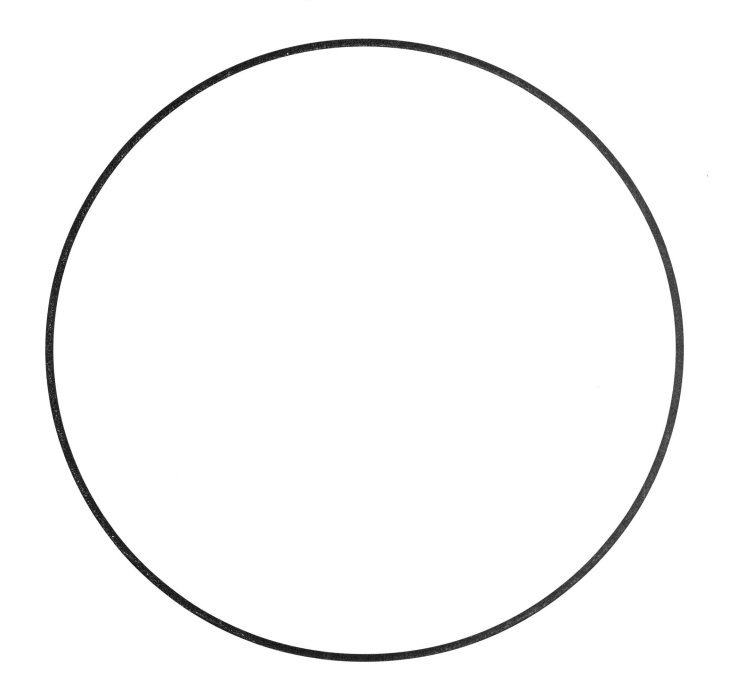

Scribble Dice Story

Color	Eyes	Mouth	Prop	Prop	Prop
2.	2.	2.	2.	2.	2.
3.	3.	3.	3.	3.	3.
4.	4.	4.	4.	4.	4.
5.	5.	5.	5.	5.	5.
6.	6.	6.	6.	6.	6.
7.	7.	7.	7.	7.	7.
8.	8.	8.	8.	8.	8.
9.	9.	9.	9.	9.	9.
10.	10.	10.	10.	10.	10.
11.	11.	11.	11.	11.	11.
12.	12.	12.	12.	12.	12.

Roll 2 DICE to figure out what Scribble you will create. Then write a story about your Scribble!

Scribble Dice Story

Color	Eyes	Mouth	Prop	Prop	Prop
2.	2.	2.	2.	2.	2.
3.	3.	3.	3.	3.	3.
4.	4.	4.	4.	4.	4.
5.	5.	5.	5.	5.	5.
6.	6.	6.	6.	6.	6.
7.	7.	7.	7.	7.	7.
8.	8.	8.	8.	8.	8.
9.	9.	9.	9.	9.	9.
10.	10.	10.	10.	10.	10.
11.	11.	11.	11.	11.	11.
12.	12.	12.	12.	12.	12.

Roll 2 DICE to figure out what Scribble you will create. Then write a story about your Scribble!

Name: _____

SCRIBBLE

Name: _____

What PEACEFUL FEELINGS can you name?

Name: _____

What ANGRY FEELINGS can you name?

Name: _____

What HAPPY FEELINGS can you name?

Name: _____

What SAD FEELINGS can you name?

Name: _____

What LOVE FEELINGS can you name?

Name: _____

What CONFIDENT FEELINGS can you name?

Name: _____

What ANXIETY FEELINGS can you name?

Peaceful

Scribble

Anger

Happiness

Sadness

Love

Confidence

Anxiety

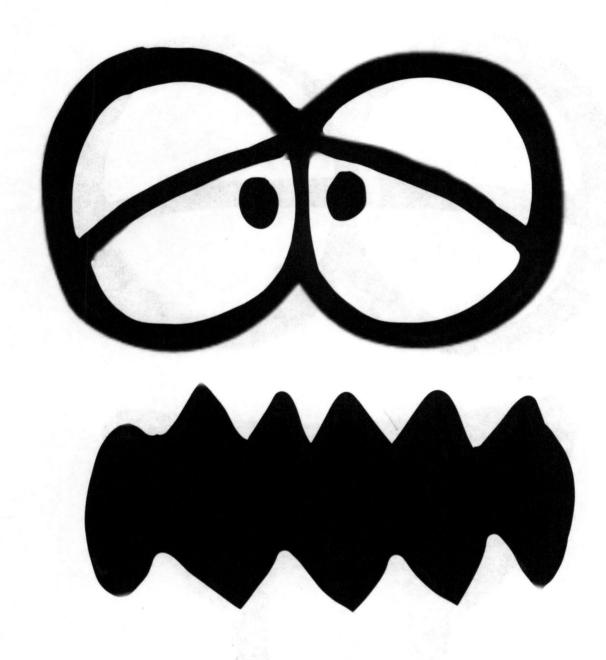

183

References:

CASEL SEL FRAMEWORK
https://casel.org/sel-framework/

COMMON CORE STANDARDS
http://www.corestandards.org/